A Trampled Flower
Can Rise Again

–Lena M. Martin–

Scriptures taken from these sources:

THE HOLY BIBLE, NEW INTERNATIONAL VERSION®, NIV® Copyright© 1973, 1978, 1984, 2010 Biblica, Inc.™ Used by permission. All rights reserved worldwide

THE GOOD NEWS BIBLE© 1994 published by the Bible Societies/ HarperCollins Publishers, Ltd. UK, Good News Bible© American Bible Society 1966, 1971, 1976, 1992. Used with permission.'

THE HOLY BIBLE, KING JAMES VERSION

ISBN 10: 0-9831459-0-3
ISBN 13: 978-0-9831459-0-5

To contact:

Lena Martin and **Rise Again Ministries**
email: youcanriseagain@gmail.com

For additional copies
visit your local bookstore or contact—

BookCentra
2673 Township Road 421
Sugarcreek, OH 44681
cservice@bookcentra.com
toll free: 877.442.6657 (877-44books)

printed by:
Carlisle Printing
OF WALNUT CREEK LTD
800.927.4196

Layout & design
by Rosetta Mullet

Jesus said: Come unto me,

all ye that labor and are heavy laden, and

I will give you rest (Matthew 11:28).

And the whole multitude sought to touch him:

for there went virtue out from him,

and healed them all (Luke 6:19).

iv | *A Trampled Flower*
can rise again

Acknowledgments

The Good Shepherd cares for His wounded sheep. My thanks and all praise to God the Father, Jesus the Son and the Holy Spirit the Comforter for the love given for me. He changes lives when it isn't in one's power to do so. I owe my all to Him.

To my dear husband Isaac, thank you for your patience through rough waters. Our faith in God has been rewarded. You gave heart when you learned of others abused in their journey. Your support to writing was a great help to me.

Love to my daughters who saw the difference the Wonderful Counselor made in your mother's life. We've seen the buds that formed and now bloom freely in our path. Girls, the sister joys you shared brought gladness to my heart, and your help in daily needs contributed to my time for writing.

Respect to my sons who coached me when I sought for answers. Hold forth the Lamp to others, passing on the Word of Life in Christ Jesus.

I am grateful to many friends who have encouraged my vision and shared hearts to reach hurting girls. Some of you have experienced abuse, and in teen years wanted help.

Thanks to my computer companion, when I needed help with the keyboard you were always there. Thanks for sharing deep but common heart struggles to express thoughts clearer.

Thanks to you who agreed to share your personal stories here. This way others are allowed to learn from your experience how God changes lives.

To you writers who have become my friends, you deserve more than words can say. How often I called on you and you readily helped me simplify and clarify the message. Thank you from deep in my heart for giving of your time to examine the manuscript and give thoughts.

God bless you dear sisters who are counseling young girls that are suffering from abuse. Press onward, giving hope to restore fragmented lives. Sharing with you brought courage to my pursuit of writing.

The Lord Jesus knows the girl who asks, seeks, and knocks with desire to know Him. She belongs to Him who made her; the Lord becomes her very own Treasure.

Thank you Rosetta Mullet for helping in the last mile of getting a book on the press. You walked patiently with me to completing the work. The hours you put into layout have proved very well.

Thanks to Rene Rivera for support and guidance given on the back cover caption. And to Mary Ellen Rivera who stood by me encouraging my vision.

Table of Contents

Introduction

A Trampled Flower Can Rise Again isn't an ordinary storybook. It is difficult for the Flower standing free in the sunlight of purity to understand the pressing guilt and fear that sexual abuse lays on the Trampled Flower.

Honest and forward attempts made to walk in the steps of the abused may be undesirable for the Healthy Flower. But for the Trampled Flower, desiring rescue from her prison of pain, it is needful to open to an understanding adult and share about the abuse.

To understand the message these pages mean to portray, please read *A Trampled Flower Can Rise Again* objectively, from beginning to end.

But everything exposed by the light becomes visible—and everything that is illuminated becomes a light (Ephesians 5:13). niv

The idea for this book was born when *Shining Light Children's Home* first opened its doors. When I met the hurting girls who came off the street, I wanted to tell them there is hope. I wanted them to know how much God cares for young girls who are devastated by the shame of sexual abuse.

There is hope!

The Lord Jesus is Love!

He is Comfort for the rejected.

He is Peace for the restless.

There are other very helpful books such as *Putting off Anger* and *Beauty for Ashes* by John Coblentz. *Beauty for Ashes* was written for a girl to open a walk through the pain of abuse.

The way to healing opened when *Beauty For Ashes* revealed the devastation abuse had done to me. I thank John Coblentz for giving God's message of healing.

I wanted to write something specifically for girls in early teens who are hidden in the confusion of sexual abuse. I could not hush the

desire in my heart to give this message of hope to young girls. I have never before written a book and have found it hard even to write a journal. It felt impossible to put the thoughts of my heart into words that someone could understand, so I asked God to help me write the thoughts of my heart.

I'd like to show young girls the path to emotional healing. I want to invite the abused girl to the comfort and freedom of our loving Lord Jesus.

In the first part of the book I aim to define sexual abuse and to make people aware of the realities of abuse.

In the last chapters, I endeavor to bring light to the process of healing. A growing young lady is like a bud opening into a beautiful flower. Sexual abuse mars and tramples these lovely buds. But all is not lost! God is big enough to restore and mend every trampled flower. Christ is the Healer and Restorer, bringing Light on the journey to wholeness.

A Trampled Flower
can rise again

My Story

The path from rejection to wholeness is my testimony. I know the despair of ruined purity. I know how it feels to live under self-accusation and fear of control.

My abuse came from someone I thought was my friend. Being four years younger, I looked up to this person as someone who understood so much more than I possibly could. My trust was betrayed.

The result of this choice turned me distant to people I had been close to. I became aimless and quiet. Work and activities seemed to be in another world apart from me. Life seemed foggy and happiness out of reach. My shame and confusion were the only things that seemed real to me.

I hated wrong and wanted right, but sinful desires held a firm grip on me. Time and again I became aware of the bondage that held me hostage, and I desperately wanted to talk with someone. I'd imagine I was talking to a pastor's wife, telling her the whole story. Then when my imagined confession faded away, I was again tormented with loneliness. Repeatedly I wondered, *Will I always live in this hopeless, solitary place of confusion?*

Four years later I accepted Christ as my Saviour. Like a prisoner released from prison, my life transformed into a new direction. The strong power of sin that had held me for so long was gone. I praised Him for the freedom I found. Living water of the Holy Spirit was the source of my life. His love was the theme of my song. This new way of living gave me hope for the future.

However, for years I felt unlovable. I wanted to be part of those around me, but a thick cloud of accusation hung over me. The distress paralyzed me. Life was simply performance without feeling.

I knew God had forgiven me, but why couldn't I forgive myself? I didn't tell anyone the experience of my past captivity to passion. I quietly kept the story to myself, repressing the pain. I didn't know how necessary it was to share my story with someone who cared. Therefore I was consumed with fear and loneliness, and kept the pain hidden deep within my heart.

But pain like that never hides completely. It always appears somewhere, usually in unexpected places. It is like hiding something deep in a closet.

As I tried my best to hide my pain, what tumbled out was unpredictable anger, from deep nagging fear.

I was scared to be honest about my fear. I hated the person I saw in the mirror and told myself, "You can **never** do anything good enough." I hurt those I lived with and wondered, "Why can't I feel love for those who are closest to me?"

I had chosen to hide my pain. This choice brought responses that were automatic, which means that while I chose the behavior, I could not choose the results. My chosen behavior was silence. The result was smothering fear and unpredictable anger.

After decades of despair I sought answers to be released from this prison. I prayed in desperation for help to love. I told my daughter there is a part of my life's story which I had never shared with anyone. I told her my social life was ruined in my young teens. In those four years, relationship skills were denied and my communication shut down. These difficulties followed me through life. When my girls heard about this, they encouraged me to find someone to help me find healing for my confused emotions.

My husband and I found kind friends who gave time for me. In prayer we invited the Lord into our presence. "Lord, come to our need—heal the pain and counsel the heart."

From the dark room of the deepest part of my heart, I told the story that had been a secret for so many years. They listened as I shared the pain I had tried to forget. I told them of my embarrassment and how vulnerable I had felt. I told of the apathy that ruled me in public because of the hopelessness that thwarted me. I shared the manipulation that had devalued my free choice. I told all I could of the lonely road I had been traveling. The wounds of my heart were exposed.

As these kind friends listened, they helped me take every sad memory to the Lord. Together we lifted our hearts in prayer, and as I unburdened my soul to God I could feel the peace of God crowding out the pain and torment that had been hidden in my heart. Christ came into that place of my heart, and with Him came quietness.

Fears that had tormented me for so long no longer had power over me. When I prayed I felt a new closeness to God. I felt a new trust that the Lord was planning the details of my life.

I will never be able to undo the damage others felt during those years of hiding my pain. I have shed many tears of regret for the harsh and angry words I gave to my family. Rebuilding those damaged relationships was slow, hard work.

I feel God's constant care while He patiently shapes me and others into His image. I am grateful the Lord searched for me in love, and did not give up on me during those years I tried to cover my grief.

God knows where you are, and I know He can help you too!

Note: All the stories in the book are true. For the protection of the characters, I have made some changes in names, details, and locations.

A Trampled Flower
can rise again

Chapter One
Muddy Waters

Lord, save us: we perish... Then he arose, and rebuked the winds and the sea; and there was a great calm. But the men marveled, saying, What manner of man is this, that even the winds and the sea obey him? (Matthew 8:25-27).

Events and Their Effects on Life's Journey

Our family needed time together, so we decided to take a week's vacation. The pelting rain didn't dampen our enthusiasm. The nine of us in the van just wanted a breath of family time. We drove along the Pacific coast, wanting to observe the great soothing swells of the vast ocean.

We crossed the Bay by way of the Golden Gate Bridge and headed still further north. We took in the greening hills of the Coastal Range. Farther on we noticed the blue ocean water was turning to a shade of brown. We had seen billows of aqua green waves rising, curling, and crashing over the sandy shore to recede into the salty deep. Now we saw the aqua sea had changed to brown. Why had the clear ocean turned to muddy waters?

Soon we approached a bridge extending over a wide river. The dark water churned beneath us as we crossed over to the other side. Now I understood why there had been a color change in the aquatic scene! The rain had disturbed the soil on the river banks along the way, washing the mire into the current until it reached the sea of seemingly endless water.

The river had grown from tributaries of smaller rills far from the ocean. Springs of the mountain, streams off slopes, waterfalls crashing over hump-backed rocks, and bubbly brooks all ran toward the great river, joining the current and destined for the sea. Each rivulet moved toward a great end: the great, wide Pacific.

Every person I meet contributes to my life, I thought, like streams add to the sea. Sometimes I cannot see or recall a specific person, but they have still added to my life experience and helped make me who I am.

There was a sad experience that deeply affected my life so long ago. Years had passed since the mid-teens when I had come as a stranger to a new setting. I lived in a whirl of many youth with new places to go every weekend. While grasping for security, someone older than I befriended me, including me in the big circle. I no longer felt "left out" with this kind of attention.

Then, on a night away from home, I was abused by this new mentor, beginning a period of emotional and mental bondage.

In my teens, there were years I wearied of the battle to retain my sanity while trapped in this sin. Then I heard the "Good News" at revival meetings: "Jesus died for you. You can be cleansed from your sin and be changed by the power of God. You can walk a new life." I saw light at the end of the dark tunnel, but it looked so very far away. It was a light of hope, however, and I held on to it tightly!

The desire to know peace and freedom followed me home. I wanted to be alone with God in the seclusion of my bedroom where I confessed my need to the Lord Jesus. "Lord Jesus, come into my heart and make it new. Shine through this terrible darkness, and wash away this heavy burden of sin. Fill my life with Your grace and power, and bring light to my path, in Jesus' name. Amen." I prayed simply.

I got up from my knees like a new person in a new world! Even the trees seemed to be rejoicing. The words of the Bible seemed to leap off the written page. Jesus was my joy. This must be the Living Waters bringing new strength to my inner being, I marveled.

I was freed from the stronghold of sin at last. But I never shared my story of painful bondage with anyone. I thought freedom in Christ was all I needed.

I accepted Jesus into my heart, but tributaries of turmoil and grief continued to muddy my life.

A Trampled Flower
can rise again

For thirty-five years hidden pain trailed me, and fear seemed to strangle me. While keeping this time of my teens a secret, inferiority often drove me to the seclusion of suffocating silence. Why the struggle with sudden anger? Why did I cause my family such emotional pain while I cared for them?

Maybe you haven't thought of a person for a long time, then something happens and the memory rushes back… a mother's gentle voice to her child brings pleasure… harsh words spark anger for justice in your heart… or a suggestive word thrown from a gang on the street causes you to blush with shame.

We ponder over a thought, and without trying it's stored in our memory.

In my early twenties I worked in a training school, caring for handicapped children. In the evenings we relaxed together, repeating quotes of the children, and sharing things that had transpired throughout the day. I deeply respected one of my co-workers because she was so serene. She had a calm spirit and an honest manner, which made it easy to talk with her. Her presence was like an ointment in the routine of work.

Relationships are part of our everyday life. Walking with friends and mingling with family requires flexibility from everyone. This is a normal part of life and helps shape us into gracious, open-hearted people. Sometimes difficult family situations can bring confusion and anxiety into our world and human tendencies make us want to withdraw from everyone to escape reality.

Even in difficult and hard to understand relationships, God knows and understands the needs of every heart. **We cannot change people, but God can.**

The fall of man in the Garden of Eden brought with it sorrow and pain that continues to this day. We cannot avoid sorrow, but we can share our burden of lamentation to God in prayer. He is the great, caring Father who is always there for us.

An emotional wound cries out for healing. Abuse that is stowed away hinders clear waters for our well-being. The beautiful aqua waters become muddy and brown with hopelessness from the betrayal we keep secret.

Hidden pain undermines our confidence to step into daily opportunities. Blame for failure can grip us with fear, making it hard to trust anyone, even in good relationships. Good friendships make life rich and full.

The world becomes a different place entering teen years, bringing fast changes. A girl hardly knows when she leaves childhood behind and learns to know herself as a new person. She has the same name as always, but she no longer knows carefree innocence.

The process of hormones brings changes to our body and emotions. It's normal to become more aware of who we are and more conscious of what others think about us. We feel a strong need for acceptance from those around us and easily focus on someone with admiration, and covet to be like them. It's all right to look for a good example, but we must realize that people will let us down because no one is perfect. God wants the first affection of our heart. In our longings for Him, we can aspire to having Him reign on the throne of our heart.

At best, it's not an easy road growing into womanhood. And for a girl who has been sexually abused it is an especially difficult time. We dare not come to the conclusion, however, that just because we have mountains of difficulty to climb, we were sexually abused at some time. Contrary to what some therapists say, one doesn't need to conclude that since she is struggling with life she must have been abused at a young age, with repressed memories. Therapists try to have you imagine you were abused and then blame your current problems on the abuse. We must not let anyone plant ideas of abuses that never happened, or imagine any sexual wrong that never happened.

An abuse victim can experience an ongoing fear that brings fruit of its own. Torments cause her to withdraw from people because she hadn't been protected in the past.

A Trampled Flower
can rise again

She thinks badly about herself, and can't love anyone else either. Having been manipulated and hurt causes her to fear control. She desperately wants relationships, but readily puts up guards for protection in given situations.

Doubts can become so big and powerful that they seemingly strangle any attempt to build relationships.

What makes me so inferior when I'm with relatives and friends? Why am I frozen with fright to be myself around them?

Why can't I bring myself to tell someone about the hands that touched me and the smooth-sounding words that were spoken to me? I was so frightened but strangely excited. Why was it so confusing?

I'm still afraid and confused, but who can I tell about it? What if my abuser discovers I have told someone? Could he or she hurt me even worse?

If there is a battle with these vicious emotions, please take heart. There *is* hope and help because Jesus cares and knows precisely what we need. He has a plan and a purpose to glorify His name.

God's Father heart sees and understands. If you are hurting, open your heart to some understanding lady with a heart after God— someone who will listen to you and will provide a safe place to voice questions and confusion. Share your pain with someone who will pray with you, and God will come to those hurting places.

If someone fails to hear, don't give up—find someone else. We need to talk and we need to give details, even if we have to cry as we release the story. By sharing it and confessing it, we no longer belong to the sad experience and the account of desolation no longer belongs to us. We can be made free from the solitude of our past.

If loneliness crushes you while this book is read, and there seems to be no one to share the path, God is still near you. He hears the words of the heart that are never said aloud. Until He brings someone to share the sorrow, pour your heart out to Him, but still seek to share the experience with someone who understands and can guide you in truth.

A Trampled Flower
can rise again

You are never alone! People have added to your life just as many streams and rivers contribute to the great Pacific Ocean. Some people have muddied your life, while others have refreshed it and soothed it. God sees all of it and covers you with the ocean of His love. His goal is to make your life full and beautiful in Him, just as the vast sea!

O thou that hearest prayer, Unto thee shall all flesh come... Which stillest the noise of the seas, the noise of their waves, and the tumult of the people (Psalm 65: 2, 7).

Prayer—

Dear Lord, sometimes life seems all mixed up and I'm so confused. But You are so great and You know everything I struggle with. Help me to see You as strong and caring in every hard experience I face. You are always with me and see the finished picture of your plan for me. Keep me in Your good purpose and show me the way to freedom. Give me a heart like Jesus while I learn to trust You today. In Jesus name, *Amen*.

*We have not a high priest which
cannot be touched with the feeling
of our infirmities (Hebrews 4:15).*

*Trust in him at all times; ye people,
Pour out your heart before him: God
is a refuge for us (Psalm 62:8).*

Activity—

God comforts us with His promises. Read Isaiah 43:2.

Are you passing through the waters of grief, fear, or some other trial today? God will walk with you through those waters.

Chapter Two
Designed By God With Great Love

*I will praise thee; for I am fearfully
and wonderfully made…*

*How precious also are thy thoughts
unto me, O God; How great is the
sum of them! (Psalm 139:14a, 17).*

Made and Known by God:
Marred by Abuse

*Early one spring morning, many years after I
came to know Jesus as Saviour, God spoke to
me. In the quietness of the dawn, a voice spoke
to me saying, "Walk through those teen years."*
"No," I said, "I don't go there."
Silence… the voice came the second time.

Again I said, "No, it's not part of my life anymore."

Silence... The third time the voice spoke, "Walk with me through those years."

Giving Him place I said, "Lord, if this is You, I will go with You through those years."

Apprehensively, I allowed my thoughts to go back to the days when I began going with the youth. Innocently, I had become trapped in a harmful relationship lasting several years.

Early that morning God spoke to me, walking with me every step through the whole story, recalling the grasp the abusive relationship had on me – being favored yet still feeling worthless and extremely lonely. Remembering how I had been betrayed by one I had trusted and looked up to, I prayed, "Please, Lord, show me my heart!" "Please, Lord, show me who I truly am, and help me escape my pain and shame."

I looked up into the face of God, and suddenly I understood. "Yes, Lord! I was a victim!" In search of friendship, I had been taken advantage of. For years, accusing thoughts had tormented me with blame for the shame I had brought on *myself. I was controlled by crippling fear and an anger that overflowed onto the ones I loved. Now, as I opened my heart to the Lord, a sense of rest and the strength of peace flowed over my wounded heart as for the first time I accepted the truth.*

My husband awoke, and listened attentively as I shared my revelation with him. I shared parts of my life I had never shared with him before. For the first time he understood the depth of the entrapment I had endured.

God cares particularly for the person He has made in you.

> *"The Lord looketh from heaven;*
> *He beholdeth all the sons of men.*
> *He fashioneth their hearts alike;*
> *He considereth all their works"*
> *(Psalm 33:13,15).*

God lovingly and carefully fitted together each part of you in your mother's belly. During the time no one saw you, you were not hidden from God. His hand was upon you even before you knew of His love.

God made us in a very intricate way. He designed a body, as well as our emotions and spirit. All this together makes us who we are. We communicate with family and friends and together we plan for the future. God planned us to be social beings, to move in interest of those near us.

Our body is very special. It is beautiful. All the parts work together in an amazing way. All day the joints of the fingers move together. The muscles of the legs and feet take us to our destination. Our arms can reach for heights, netting a butterfly swaying above us. All these parts were wisely designed by our Creator.

The body is the first way people get to know who we are. They see our face, our bright eyes, or our winsome smile and notice how tall we are. Later they get to know what comes from our heart, those invisible parts of us—how we feel

about things, and what we like and don't like. But our body is visible right away.

Our emotions are a part of us we can't see, but our body sometimes shows our emotions. For example, when we feel sad we might cry, or when we're happy, our mouth and lungs make the sound of laughter. Our spirit is the invisible but conscious being that God placed in our body. It is the part of us that God values the most and will someday go to be with God when we die.

The body and feelings work together very closely. When we love people, we are kind to them by helping them with our hands or hugging them with our arms. This is the way we show what we feel inside. It works the other way too. When someone does something to our body, we feel a certain way inside about it. If someone slaps us, we will feel angry or sad inside. If someone rubs our hand or pats our shoulder, we feel comforted and loved inside.

There are parts of the body that are so special and private they belong only to the person who lives in that body. They are hers and God's. They are for no one else to see. Every part of the girl that God made is beautiful and wonderful. Some parts are too special to share with anyone except one special man, and that is her husband.

If someone suggests uncovering private areas, or exposes some of his or her own they with impure desires want to control you. If someone gives a suggestive word or feels the breasts, or touches the legs with intentions to move toward the personal area, it is confusing because the body likes being touched. Doubtful feelings, however, say it is wrong for that person to touch. The offender may even say nice things to deceive. People like this act a lie to win favor and work out their hurtful pleasure. This is called sexual abuse. This is what it means to be molested. Emotions are hurt and confused, and talking about it seems impossible and scary.

Down in the most secret place of the heart, where only the girl and God are, she doesn't feel right about it. There are conflicting signals because the body was made to feel good with touch. But God said it's only hers and God's.

Even when it seems she can't ever, ever get away from the pain of the wound hidden deep in

her heart, God sees and cares. God knows and is still near the girl who has been sexually abused. He hears the cry of the heart and sees the tear slipping from the eyes. Actually, He cries too, because He is sad too about things that hurt.

It takes courage to tell someone about the pain and shame. What if they don't believe what we say? What if we find it impossible to tell because there are no words to explain the feeling? It's like taking a scab off a sore that isn't healed—it hurts all over again. Jesus understands all of these feelings.

I want to assure you, a girl can turn those feelings over to God. Remember, God made that darling little baby that was you, and He loves you still—now!

In the dark of evening His sight is not dimmed. When everything seems like night and we're alone, He is light around us—even when we can't see the light.

Prayer—

Dear Lord Jesus, You are Light. There is no darkness in You. You understand everything about me. You understand everything I can't seem to say. You know all the sadness I feel, and You see and understand my tears. Help me to be kind and not angry, to love and not hate. Help me to find someone who understands my story and listens while I try to tell my mixed-up feelings. I want to feel love in my heart for You. In Jesus' name, *Amen*.

In my distress I cried unto the LORD,
and he heard me (Psalm 120:1).

O LORD my God, thou art very great…
Who coverest thyself with light as
with a garment (Psalm 104:1a,2a).

The darkness and the light are both
alike to thee (Psalm 139:12b).

How precious also are thy thoughts unto
me, O God: How great is the sum of them!
If I should count them, they are more in
number than the sand: When I awake,
I am still with thee (Psalm 139:17,18).

Whom having not seen, ye love; in
whom, though now ye see him not, yet
believing, ye rejoice with joy unspeakable
and full of glory (I Peter 1:8).

Activity—

1. Go outside and feel the sun's warmth. God's love is like that. It's all around you!

2. Pick up sand or fine stones. Can you count sand on the shore? God has that many, and more, good thoughts about you.

3. What good thoughts could He be thinking of you right now?

Psalm 139

Nancy
Finds Real Love at Last

Nancy wants to forget what happened to her when she was a little girl. She craves love from friends around her. But she is afraid to respond to the love they give.

Before Nancy met friends who love Jesus, she would go to bed hungry, cold, and scared. Her mother spent much of her time at the bar on the block or with other acquaintances on the street. With no one's protection, Nancy was sexually harassed. Nancy's mother often came home feeling bad, and sometimes Nancy and her sister suffered beatings as she screamed at them.

One day Mother took Nancy's sister along to show her how to earn money as a prostitute. In fright, the poor young girl ran home to escape schemes of that sort.

In almost constant fear, they ran to Grandmother's house, "We want to live with you, Grandma. We're afraid because that man wants to hurt us," said Nancy.

"We can hide in your house," said Nancy's sister. "Then when Mama's drunk she can't hurt us, and she can't take me away where they will hurt me."

"Oh, you dear girls," Grandmother sympathized. "I will do what I can."

Grandmother wanted to protect them, but she soon became too ill to care for them. She took them to a house for children in town, but before long she was too weak to visit them.

In desperation, the girls ran away from the children's home to find her. Darting through her house, they ran out the back door and found the back yard also empty.

"Where is Grandmother?" wailed Nancy.

Abandoned and forgotten by their mother, and with their grandmother who cared about them now ill and in the hospital, they would have to fend for themselves.

To avoid further failure, Nancy decided to be tough and not need anyone's help. Life was fearful on those lonely streets; noisy boys lurked in the darkness.

"If they come near, I will kick them hard," Nancy vowed from her hiding place.

A man staggered and slumped to the ground nearby. The sisters clung together, fearful of what lurked in the shadows.

At daybreak, street children clamored around the trash heap. Nancy and her sister also looked through the debris for a bite to quiet their hunger.

A social worker walked up to talk with the two ragged girls trudging around the dump.

"Girls, there is a place here in town with good food and a place to sleep with other children. Will you ride with me to see it?"

With kind persuasion the social worker led the girls to her car. Driving through town they came to a fenced area around a large white house. She opened the gate for their entrance and talked with the manager. The girls were left to discover the needs of an understaffed home with a nearly empty pantry and bare kitchen cupboards.

One day a kind woman named Eva visited the orphanage. "These children need someone to fix food for them," she said. "They are hungry."

Nancy followed at a distance as Eva moved toward the gate. The children clung to her as she prepared to leave.

The next day Eva brought Reba along to prepare a big lunch of rice and beans.

"We need to come more often to prepare dinner in the kitchen for these hungry children," suggested Reba, the little ones clamoring around her.

When lunch was ready, Nancy would not eat with anyone in the dining room. When everyone was eating, she would go to a far corner in another room, where someone would find her and give her a plate of food, which she ate contentedly in solitude.

In time Nancy ventured closer to the kind ladies. She reached for Reba's cell phone. A smile lit her face when she punched numbers and it beeped in her ear.

The other children were soon playing games and running races under Eva's supervision. When it was time for Eva and Reba to leave, the children followed close, wanting hugs, while begging them to come back the next day.

"We'll come back tomorrow at lunch time," Eva called over her shoulder.

When anyone talked to her, Nancy answered loudly and offensively, running away. She found it impossible to be pleasant and loving; she was so overcome by fear that someone might hurt her again. Her mother had always degraded her, and her grandmother had dropped her off at a strange place. She was afraid something even worse might happen. She would make herself strong, she decided. She would hurt others so she would not get hurt herself.

One day someone took her to the doctor. He gave medication to calm her down, but the poor girl still acted like a scared little rabbit.

A new Christian Children's Home had opened on the other side of town and it was there that Eva and Reba helped homeless boys and girls, giving them beds, clean clothes, and yummy food to eat. The older children went to school while the younger ones played and shared toys. Helpful Christian ladies cared for them every day.

One day a car pulled up to the home where Nancy and her sister lived. "We have come to take Nancy and her sister to a new home," they heard the social worker say as she talked with the manager inside the fence.

At the new home Nancy's sister sat with the other girls on the sofa looking at a story book, but Nancy ran to a quiet corner of the house to be alone.

One day the girls combed through Nancy's long, dark hair. As she sat still for a little bit, Clara put pretty clasps in her hair.

"Nancy, you look lovely!" her friends exclaimed. Seeming not to notice, Nancy hopped off the chair and ran away. Picking up a stick, she dragged it to make marks in the ground.

When Nancy was taken to the doctor again, the medication for her restlessness was discontinued. Workers wanted to be a friend, but sometimes her mixed-up feelings still controlled her. She acted as if she didn't notice people around her, and made no effort to be polite and pleasant with them. Could she ever get away from the crushing pain she felt deep inside?

Workers patiently guided Nancy through her needs.

A Trampled Flower can rise again

"Come to the sofa for a story." Loving arms reached around her rigid body while a kind voice read stories. She sat quietly. She loved Bible stories and listened with rapt attention.

Eventually Nancy's activity became more relaxed. Instead of trying to escape her friends, it was easier to talk with them and join in games with the children.

"What will we do today?" she asked as she sat at the table with the others and ate breakfast with them.

Nancy loved to listen when older people spoke. She was learning that she belonged to someone, and that it was safe with God and His people who cared about her. They accepted her even if she was imperfect, and this made her feel valued. God's love was softening the little girl's heart that had once been frozen with fear.

One morning after breakfast when chores were done, the children ran along outside. The sun wove lacy shadows through the trees along the curved path that led to school.

Inside the classroom, the teachers were preparing lessons for the new day. "Good morning," said Teacher Susan, as Nancy and other children found their desks and sat down.

They sang three songs, then Teacher Susan told a story about Jesus. This morning she talked about the time He calmed the stormy waters after He was wakened by His disciples who were in the boat with Him.

"Bless us today and direct us in your way," Teacher Susan prayed.

After devotion time the children reached for their workbooks, but not Nancy. She was busy drawing an ugly picture of Teacher Susan.

Earlier in the week, Susan had asked Nancy to work harder on lessons. Teacher Susan knew Nancy was smart and could do better work. But this made Nancy feel controlled and shameful again. Her mother had told her that she could never be anything good, and now she knew it was true, and she hated herself and her teacher.

When Teacher Susan saw the picture Nancy was drawing, Nancy tore up her exam paper, stepped on it, and threw her pencil on the floor.

"Nancy, you will need to go to the next room for time out," Teacher Susan spoke sadly.

A Trampled Flower
can rise again

Alone in that room, Nancy found a tissue box and tore the tissues into bits. Then she sat still, all mixed-up inside, angry at everything and everyone. She felt so alone and scared.

Nancy remembered the Bible stories she loved so much. She thought of the time Jesus healed the man who had been blind from birth. She remembered the story where Jesus made the girl who died live again and her mother was so very happy. She knew Jesus loved her now too, even in her loneliness and nastiness.

Nancy thought of kind Teacher Susan; Teacher never yelled or hit her. She had seen the love in Susan's sad eyes when she left Nancy in the quiet room.

Nancy found a piece of paper and quickly wrote a note: "*I love you very much, Teacher Susan. From Nancy.*" Walking to the classroom she handed it to the teacher.

Teacher Susan put her arms around her and smiled. "I love you too, very much, Nancy."

The rest of the day seemed to bloom. The sunlight seemed more cheery as it shone through the classroom windows. Warm feelings radiated love to her friends and teacher.

Nancy is older now, but still finds an empty spot in her heart that cries for Mother. Sharing is a big part of her life. She beckons children to sing "God is so good" and they join in her fun games. The pain of rejection as a child lingers, but she sees she is not the only hurting person, and God walks with her through that sorrow.

Questions—

1. Why did Nancy struggle with relationships?

2. When she opened her heart to accept love from her caregivers, was there a change to what she could give others?

Chapter Three
God Is Here

Jesus Christ is the same yesterday and today and forever (Hebrews 13:8).

Taking the Reason for Guilt is Not Always the Answer

In a winter storm, dark clouds roll across the sky. Raindrops pelt roof tops, crash on trees, and splash into puddles. We make a dash for the house through the rain and get drenched. A prayer of thanks rises as we watch the downpour on arid land.

Sunbeams streak across the opening sky. Pebbles glimmer clean, nestled in mounds of earth. Leaves clean from dust, flutter in the air. Masses of awesome bright orange poppies and blue lupines cover mountain slopes in the Los

Padres mountain range.

A rainbow arches through the vapor in a ribbon of lavender, deep purple, blue, green, yellow, orange, and red.

The rainbow is a reminder of a promise God made to man long ago to never flood the earth again. When God speaks, you know He is not slack keeping His promises. We can find ourselves in a habit of wrong thinking but our God is wisdom and has never changed. We can focus beyond our human limitations to the Creator of earth and sky. He has no boundaries.

A year passed since my early morning talk with God. It was March again, and the green of the season covered the usual brown hills of southern California. Flowering trees of lavender, white and pink showed their beauty from front lawns and sidewalks. I accompanied my husband to an auction on that beautiful spring day. While he attended the auction, I enjoyed quiet, comfortable moments with God alone in the van on the auction parking lot. What a cool, refreshing spring day that was.

In meditation and prayer, I sought to know God better. "I want to trust you during difficult times for your praise," I prayed. "Help me bless others in undesirable experiences of life as well as joyful times; help me find a yielded heart when it is my lot to walk through pain."

Recently I again expressed sudden anger; and I longed for a heart reflecting more of Jesus.

I sought God to direct the days ahead giving my life to Him anew. As I read <u>My Utmost for His Highest</u> by Oswald Chambers, commitment worked in my heart," God wants me; not what I can do." From that day, I wanted to remember the blessing of waiting on the Lord to fill my need.

An abused girl should be careful about putting the blame on herself. Taking the guilt to free another feels unselfish. Such reason seems like humility, but truth will always stand. Truth cannot be changed. She feels shame for what happened, but she was betrayed. Someone cheated her of her purity and so the burden of guilt does not belong to her.

Her abuser may have used different ways to trick her. He may have told her, "You are a pretty girl." Or he may have said, "I want to love you." Maybe he said he is lonely and needed a friend, venturing into private places, or exposing of his own for his shameful lust.

An abuser can be someone she sees every day. He may be nice when other people are around. He might be religious or even pray with a group. He may try to cover his sin by doing other good things. But remember that good deeds can never cover sin.

Feelings of failure are understandable, but she was taken advantage of. She may know who molested her as a child, but now she wants to be pure and free. But the pain of the abuse takes control, and shows itself in unpredictable times in emotions of anger and fear. The outcome of her expression confuses her.

In her present day, her thoughts continually excuse others, and by her reasoning heaps the

blame for mistakes and discord on herself. With her heart full of self condemning thoughts, words tumble from her mouth of the same to others.

She can hurt so much it's hard for her to know what truth really is. God wants to take the blame away. Believing a lie brings bondage, truth sets her free.

When the beauty of purity is trampled on by selfish and rude people, she cannot feel joy, love, or pity for people around her; her thoughts are locked in a lie. God is waiting to free her.

Jesus knows the truth about everything that happened. As she remembers and shares her abuse she can be guided to truth. God can even lead the abuser in truth to find the help he needs.

While the sunshine of love shows through the mist of trials, the rainbow of promise lights the path. Warm rays draw minerals into the root of plants. So it is with the light of God's Word. The Bible gives nutrients that revive our thirsty souls. The promises in His word are true, always! They are for you right now.

Favorite verses—

Casting all your care upon him; for
he careth for you (1 Peter 5:7).

If ye then, being evil, know how to give
good gifts…how much more shall your
Father which is in heaven give good things
to them that ask Him? (Matthew 7:11).

But He will with the temptation also make
a way to escape… (1 Corinthians 10:13b).

Greater is He that is in you, than he
that is in the world (I John 4:4b).

With men this is impossible; but with God
all things are possible (Matthew 19:26b).

Prayer—

Dear Jesus, I praise You for your love that never changes. You love me today the same as You did yesterday, last year, and even before I was abused. Keep me from evil and from things that displease You. Help me to show Your pure love to others. Help me to remember You are near me all the time. You are my hiding place and my Strong Helper at all times. In Jesus' name,

Amen.

Activity—

Find more promise verses and write them in a notebook.

Jean
Finds the Answer

When Jean's family moved to their new house, her family thought the bachelor that lived next door was a kind, lonely man. No one imagined he'd hurt their little girls — especially not a five-year-old.

Moving days were busy days. Dad and his helpers loaded the truck with furniture and boxes. A friend held baby Clinton while Mama marked "kitchen" on the boxes.

"Our friends have made moving day a lot easier," she said. "Thanks so much for your help!"

Jean and Sarah took Clinton to the car. Soon the loaded cars and trucks traveled to the new house.

"It's nice of Ray to rent his house to us," said Mama. "He lives in the same yard and has no family. Now he won't be alone."

"Does Ray go to church?" Jean asked when she saw their new landlord outside the house.

"Yes, he has a car and goes to church," said Mama. "He is glad to eat meals at our house. He will eat food that is better for him when he eats with a family."

Before long, the new house began to feel like home. Ray came over for dinner every day. Finding a chair in the living room, he sat down while Mama busily prepared food. Since Sarah was away at school, Ray was alone with Jean. He said nice things to her, saying he wanted to be her friend.

Jean told him she was going to school next year. "You will be a smart girl," he said, smiling. "Come here to me." He held Jean close, rubbing her leg. Jean didn't know why he felt her leg like that. His hands felt rough and his heavy breathing was very close.

The next day Ray came into the house early again. "How is my little girl?" he asked Jean.

Mama was in the kitchen baking bread. The delicious aroma from the warm oven filled the air. Ray called Jean over to him. He held her close and massaged her legs again. Something about this closeness did not feel right! Why did Ray do this to her? Daddy never acted like that. The next day when he beckoned her to come to him, he did more than rub her legs. He reached inside her underwear and touched her where nobody should touch. It sent tingling feelings through her body. Jean wanted to scream for Mama, but in some ways it felt good to be loved. Deep down she knew something was wrong.

Before they moved to this new house, Jean had talked to Mama about everything. Now Ray had done the same kind of things to Sarah, her younger sister. Why didn't their parents do something to stop him?

Do other men touch little girls where it should be private? Why did Mama and Daddy not see what Ray was doing to her and take care it didn't happen again? All these questions tumbled around in her young mind. The damage of being cheated made it hard to tell Mama. She longed to tell her about it, but would she listen and believe her story?

Jean felt alone. Ray's squalid attention marred the purity God put into every child. She felt tricked and used. Her world of innocence was

A Trampled Flower
can rise again

crushed. Her childhood dream of being Daddy's princess was shattered. All the tiny pieces settled in her wounded heart.

A new school year began and Jean went to first grade. School opened a new world of friends and opportunities. She excelled academically and found new purpose in working hard to earn good grades. That eased the pain in her heart just a little.

Jean wanted to feel safe, but her world felt frightfully overwhelming. Wanting to calm her anxiety, she turned to food for comfort. Jean was bothered by her weight problem. She hated herself for eating so much. She wanted to be slim like other girls in her class. When unkind boys teased her it added to the pain that was already in her heart.

After a few years, Jean's family moved again, but she continued to feel fearful and uncertain. When she was with others, she tried to hide her real feelings with laughter and fun. Her bubbly personality drew many friends. But would they like her if they knew what had happened? Had she tempted Ray to do what he did?

How could she keep living with all these unanswered questions? Where was God? She wanted to feel close to Him. Why was she so restless and unable to feel His peace? Someone had trampled on the pure, sweet flower that God had created Jean to be. She felt guilty and dirty. When anxiety overwhelmed her, she felt driven to masturbation. Then she hated herself for doing it again and again. How could she ever quit?

Jean took all the lingering memories of Ray, buried them down deep inside and refused to think about them. *Now I want to live like other girls. They have lots of fun and do wonderful things like birthday parties and boat rides. I'm going to forget the pain inside and enjoy life as my friends seem to.*

Sometime later Jean received Jesus as her personal Saviour. The heavy burden of guilt was lifted as she opened her heart to his presence.

A Trampled Flower can rise again

When Jean was nineteen, she met a fine young man that she could trust. When she met Thomas, Jean saw him as a real gentleman. Ever since she had become a Christian, she had prayed that God would lead her to a wonderful Christian man that she could trust and who would listen to her heart. She was delighted when Thomas chose her for his bride and anticipated many happy years together.

Family and friends gathered to share in their joy on that beautiful wedding day. Jean and Thomas vowed to be faithful to each other for the remainder of their lives. They were committed to each other's highest good. God had led them together and many wishes of happiness were expressed by the guests.

Jean longed to love Thomas fully as God wanted her to. She wanted to enjoy marital intimacy but a nameless fear haunted her and seemed to destroy all her best intentions to be sexually free with her husband.

Jean felt confused and guilty. *Something must be wrong with me,* she thought. *How can I give affection when I feel so unlovely? Must I live in pretense all my life, acting as if everything is fine, while my heart feels broken into a thousand pieces?* The damage of abuse suppressed any hope of freedom to love.

After many years of difficulty, Jean allowed herself to look at the painful memories that she had locked up so tightly. She and Thomas went to a seminar for sexually abused people.

During the seminar, they watched a video of a molested girl sharing her story of abuse. Tears ran down Jean's cheeks as she realized her inner pain came from being sexually abused by neighbor Ray when she was only five and six years old. All the memories flooded back and once again she shuddered as she remembered those rough hands and the heavy breathing. The effects of that untold abuse had followed her all these years and filled her with confusion, regret, and anguish.

God wanted to restore Jean to a beautiful blooming flower again. She found kind Christian friends who let her tell her story of pain and prayed with her. With God's help and her friends' support, Jean brought all those deep, aching hurts to God and forgave Ray for the damage he had done to her. Freedom came to Jean's heart when she unlocked those bad memories and looked honestly at what had happened.

God replaced her tears of shame and hurt with the joy of pure love! She found Jesus to be the Friend who loves at all times. Now God's love can flow through her heart to others. He can heal the broken heart and make it whole again.

Today, instead of trying to find comfort in food or self abuse, Jean tells Jesus about her pain and disappointments. She finds comfort, rest, and peace in His tender love. She is also able to love and trust her husband Thomas more than ever before. Now that she has experienced this part of healing in her own heart, she tells other abused women about the freedom and peace that Jesus gives to a thirsty heart. A trampled flower CAN bloom again! It has exquisite beauty and heavenly fragrance because of the healing Jesus brings.

Questions—

1. How did Jean feel when she couldn't tell anyone what Ray had done to her?

2. Did putting the memory of abuse behind locked doors bring freedom to her?

3. Since Jean couldn't make her pain go away on her own, how did she find healing?

It's ok to hurt.
Jesus hurt.

On the power of healing…
    He let Himself feel hurt;
So you know He understands what hurt is.

Jesus is the *Forgiver.*
He is the *Healer.*
He is the *Comforter.*

To be healed you must allow hurt to be okay,
And bring the truth of the pain to the
Divine Healer.

To ignore it or refuse it can hinder what God
wants to do for you. He wants to show you His
Father heart.

A Trampled Flower
can rise again

Chapter Four
He Makes the Desert a Garden

*The Lord will guide you always; he will
satisfy your needs in a sun-scorched
land and will strengthen your frame.*

*You will be like a well-watered
garden, like a spring whose waters
never fail (Isaiah 58:11 niv).*

Being Transparent about Abuse

Here in the Southwest, deserts receive little
rain for most of the year. Only during the winter
months is there any moisture to speak of. Instead
of hibernating in the winter, desert wildlife
becomes dormant in the hot, dry summers. The
spade-foot toad, desert tortoise, Gila monster,

and other lizards bury themselves in the sand during the hottest part of the day.

In the cooler months of the year when moisture arrives, the plants bud to new life. Pools are nesting places for spawning of the spade-foot toad. In a few days, tadpoles grow legs and hop beyond the pools. During this season of progress and growth, desert creatures become more active in their sandy habitat.

It was a year since the day of meditation in the auction parking lot. I shared for the first time with my oldest daughter at home how a relationship in my teens held me in seclusion for four years. "I couldn't develop social skills," I said. "I think that's why I struggle now."

A few weeks later we met together. It was family time for refreshment and bonding with our children, at the house of our married son. Having known my struggles, our older sons and daughters asked to have a special time to engage in talking. I consented gladly. The times for real sharing were rare. While we gathered in a room, they kindly and gently told of their love for me. Their care caused my tears to flow. They

told me they would like to see me get help by sharing with someone. In tearful gratitude I told them I needed to talk with someone, and I want help.

My son gave me the book Beauty for Ashes to read. The next morning I had an opportunity to read it when my husband left early to go out for breakfast with the men at work. Later my son asked if I read the book and if I liked it. I said it just made me cry. He said that was because I had a wound that was scabbed over but not healed.

How I longed for total healing for my wounded soul!

Life can feel like a desert, dry with defeat and parched with rejection. Hiding in the sand is impossible, and there is little hope for things to get better. An abused girl suffers the ongoing effects of this sin done against her.

When God made each of us, He said, "It is very good!" God has a good plan for each of us, but the devil wants to hurt and destroy us.

Perhaps a teacher or a youth group leader asked wrong things of a girl, or asked untactful questions. Perhaps they spread rumors or exposed her sad secrets to others who didn't need to know. They may have spoken of or exposed sexual activity. Being defrauded in such a situation, she felt defenseless. With a feeling of worthlessness, maybe she let it happen again. Now she feels unloved because she can't love. Emotions like this are an all-too-common result of being molested and abused.

It appears easiest to hush up about it. But while the girl wants to suppress the memory, she wonders why she is locked in a mode of painful defeat and mistrust. If she does not talk about her abuse with someone she can trust, the hurt will burrow deeper inside. The hidden pain will keep her from living freely in God's garden of girls.

Jesus feels very sad when a girl suffers so deeply from someone's sin. He loves her very much and knows she has been cheated. He feels those bruises that cause her to conclude she is of no value. He knows the bitterness she feels from failure.

It is not true when others say it's okay for men to do sexual acts with girls. This is false and wrong and it leaves a wound no one else can see.

When a father uses his daughter for his own sexual pleasure, something inside her dies. The longing for Father's protection and guidance is now hurt and bruised. She feels the aching void of his abuse, causing deep feelings of father hunger. When she sees a man, she asks herself, *is this man someone I can trust? Is this someone who would protect me? Or would he use his power to hurt me?*

Purity is beautiful, and clean thoughts are a "Well of Life." A girl can spoil this beauty by following lustful desires to secretly fondle another girl's body. She does a great hurt to that girl and to herself. This is homosexual behavior, and it is wrong. It will turn a girl's life into a lonely, parched desert.

God wants girls in His palace of purity. He wants them free to love friends in a pure way.

Sometimes girls try to bring sexual pleasure to their own body. This is called masturbation, and it is sinful. God designed sex to be between a husband and wife, not one person alone. When a girl stimulates herself sexually, she is focusing on herself and trying to fill the emptiness in her heart. Sexual pleasure will never fill that emptiness. Any girl who is tempted to masturbate should talk to God about it. She should also seek direction and find help from someone who understands.

To begin healing from incest, homosexuality, or masturbation, a girl must open her disquieted heart before God and share her story with a mature Christian lady. No matter what has happened or what was done, God has a plan for purity, and He makes it possible to be whole and pure in every part of life.

Believing truth makes Satan's power crumble!

How can we prepare our hearts to be a ready garden for good seed? A yielded heart is good soil for the Master Gardener. To begin to see how good God is and how much we need Him is the

A Trampled Flower
can rise again

beginning of preparing the garden of our heart. With eyes of faith on the light of His face, living water can refresh us in the desert.

Life can bloom and flourish just as a flower garden gives sweet fragrance. With thirst for truth and eyes of faith, God prepares a nutritious table before us in the midst of trouble. The soul can be restored, walking hand in hand with Jesus.

Wherever life takes us, He can transform a desert into a watered garden as He forms the flowers of patience and kindness in our way.

*The LORD is good, a strong hold in
the day of trouble; and he knoweth
them that trust in him (Nahum 1:7).*

*They will be like a well-watered garden,
and they will sorrow no more.
I will turn their mourning into gladness;
I will give them comfort and joy instead
of sorrow (Jeremiah 31:12b,13b niv).*

*I will even make…rivers in the
desert (Isaiah 43:19 nkjv).*

Prayer—

Dear Jesus, I need your constant love and care. You see how I struggle against wrong in my life, and still You love me. Help me trust You when it's not easy, because nothing is too hard for You. Thank you for your mercy and kindness. It's like a spring of water in my desert. Teach me your ways. Help me find someone I can trust who can help me with the hard, confusing questions in my heart. I give my desert heart to You. Make it a lovely garden for your glory and your praise. In Jesus' name, *Amen.*

Activity—

Read Psalm 94. Who will stand up for me against those who do wrong?

Psalm 94:17 Unless the Lord had been my help, my soul had almost dwelt in silence.

The Mystery
of Myra's Sad Eyes

Myra was the smartest girl in class, but she was very shy – and her eyes were so hauntingly sad. *I'd like to get to know her better,* Arlene thought.

"Mother," Arlene asked one day, "Could we visit the Smiths? They are the new family that moved onto the farm down the road. Myra Smith sits beside me on the bus. She and her brother are very smart, but they are so quiet and don't seem to have many friends.

"Yes, I would like to meet Myra's mother. Maybe Daddy could take us to their house on Saturday," Mother responded.

Saturday morning Arlene mixed a batch of sugar cookies and baked them in the hot oven. Soon rows of finished cookies cooled on the counter.

"Could we take some cookies to Myra's house?" Arlene wondered.

"That's a great idea," Mother agreed. "You may put them into the tin box with the snow scene on the lid."

Arlene and her sister Patricia carefully placed the sugar cookies into the tin. "M-m-m, they look so yummy!" said Patricia.

"And that is the prettiest tin box," exclaimed Arlene. "I think Myra will like it, and her brother will enjoy the cookies too."

When the family was in the car ready to go, Arlene carefully held the tin box of cookies. They drove over the hill and turned in the lane beside a pasture where some cows were grazing.

"Myra said they milk twelve cows every morning before school. They get up very early to do their chores!"

Father stopped at the front door to let Mother and the girls off. "I'll be back in a little while," he said, then drove away to do an errand.

Hearing the knock, Myra's mother opened the door. "Come in," she said smiling.

Myra stood shyly as her mother offered a chair to her visitor. There weren't enough chairs for everyone to sit down, so the girls sat on a bed nearby. The bare walls and echoing sounds showed little furnishings.

"We baked some cookies for you," said Arlene, handing the tin to Myra's mother.

"Thank you," she exclaimed. "What a pretty box! You are so very thoughtful."

The girls sat quietly while their mothers visited. The three girls glanced at one another. Soon Myra got up and the girls followed her outside. They leaned on the railing of the porch and chatted about school. Sometime later Father drove up.

"Daddy is here," called Arlene. While good-byes were said and smiles were shared they scampered down the steps, and with a wave they drove away.

"Mrs. Smith was very nice to us," said Mother. "But she seemed sad, and they are quite poor. I'm glad my girls made friends with our neighbors."

"Sometimes Myra looks like she has been crying when she gets on the bus," said Arlene. Her brother, Henry, always sits quietly on the seat across from Myra. He seems so pleasant and is very polite."

The next Monday when Myra got on the bus, Arlene smiled and scooted over on the seat to make room for her. Myra sat quietly beside her.

"What did you do yesterday?" asked Arlene, hoping to start a conversation.

"We were all at home," answered Myra.

"Did you go to church?"

"Sometimes we go to church, but not every Sunday," said Myra.

Several days later, Arlene heard Father ask Mother, "Did you hear what happened to the Smiths?"

"No," what happened?"

"The police wanted Mr. Smith to come out of the house so they could arrest him. He was abusing Myra," Father said soberly.

"Oh, no. What did they do?"

"The police stood outside the house with guns and commanded Mr. Smith to come out to them. He didn't want to because he knew he was in trouble with the law. He was committing incest with Myra. He was scared and didn't want to see the police. He had a gun and killed himself."

"What a tragedy. How disappointed and traumatized Myra and all of them must be," Mother spoke in shock.

"What do you mean he was abusing Myra?" Arlene asked her mother later. "

"Myra's father was touching her in ways and places for his own sexual pleasure. God has a good and beautiful plan for the home, and He designed husbands and wives to bring pleasure to each other. It is wrong for fathers or other relatives to abuse girls, even if they are in the same family. When a father or brother does this to a girl in the family, it is called incest. I feel so sorry for Myra. She will suffer terrible emotional trauma because her father violated her body and used what didn't belong to him. Now we know why she often seemed so sad. Poor, poor Myra."

Mother continued, "I feel sorry for Myra. She must feel like discarded trash on a rubbish pile. Girls who go through such experiences are trapped in loneliness, their wounded soul humiliated. In rejection they despair ever being normal again."

"God planned that girls would have strong, loving fathers to take care of them as they grow up. When a young lady marries, God designed sex to be part of that special bond with her husband. If a selfish father sexually takes what belongs to her future husband, the girl fears control because God's design for her body was marred."

"A girl needs a father who smiles when she laughs. She wants him to talk with her and be interested in her life, giving good advice about friendships. When a girl like Myra finds out that her father is actually a selfish, cruel man, she longs for a real father," Mother went on.

"She feels confused about men because she wants to be treasured by a man as her father should have done, but she fears that all men are like her selfish father. She is both attracted to, and scared of men. This confusion keeps her from being free with people, and it makes her behave in ways that even she doesn't understand."

The good thing about this sad life is that God is just waiting to be a good, loving Father to her. She can open her heart to Him and He will take her close to Himself. She can talk to Jesus about her disappointments and loneliness, and she will find that He really loves her with a Father-heart.

God loves girls like Myra very much and will be the Father they dream about. Jesus reaches out to all hurting women and offers His friendship and care.

Questions—

1. How do you think Myra felt when she couldn't share as she sat beside Arlene on the bus?

2. How do you think Myra felt when Arlene was visiting her house?

3. Read about Jesus' love in I John 4:19. Where does love begin? Write the verse on paper and put it where you will see it every day.

And (I) will be a Father unto you, and ye shall be my sons and daughters, saith the Lord Almighty (II Corinthians 6:18).

Chapter Five
Treasured By God While Trampled By Man

Lord, all my desire is before thee; and my groaning is not hid from thee" (Psalm 38:9).

Treasured by God While *Trampled* by Man

Santa Ana winds sweep mercilessly over the Pacific coastal mountains, touching everything on the way. Trees bend with gusts of harsh wind. Tumble-weeds roll along, bouncing, crashing into walls, joining a mass of their kind.

Other times lesser winds cause leaves to flutter, while flowers nod their heads in rhythm with everything around them. All nature sways in the silent symphony of the Maker.

Can our heart flow with the same kind of peace in any occurring circumstances? Or does it more often feel like a harsh storm? Abuse of any kind can make our hearts feel worn and battered.

When my family was together at our son's house, they in love recommended I share my story with someone. It brought a sense of relief to know help was coming my way. I was waiting for someone to make the appointment with our friends for a special time of sharing.

But my family was waiting for me to plan the set time to talk, on my own.

Then it happened again, ridiculous and abrupt—an expression of anger spilled out suddenly for no real reason. My husband had a plan: He wanted to put up a mini barn for guests when "extra space" was needed. Sometimes our large seven-bedroom house was filled when guests came to bless us. At that time we had seven children at home.

His suggestion of a mini cabin surprised me. To myself I thought, I'm satisfied the way it is. Can't he see I'm content and that I gave that need over to the Lord?

A Trampled Flower
can rise again

"I'm not looking for more room!" I burst out. "Can't you see I'm content the way we have it?"

Moments later I was filled with deep regret. I hurried to find my husband and told him how sorry I was. "Your suggestion is fine," I told him. "I don't like being this way! When can I go for help?"

"How about Saturday?" he suggested.

When my daughters heard about our plans, they offered to stay with the children of the couple we planned to meet with so they could have more free time with my husband and me.

There are times when we feel our friends don't like us. We want to be loved but we can't trust anyone. Maybe we are so overwhelmed with sadness and our hearts are so heavy with pain that we scarcely care what happens around us.

Perhaps we planned to travel with friends, but the trip was canceled. Like harsh winds, confusion rose up within us. We see others respond graciously to disappointment and we wonder, *What's wrong with me? Will I ever feel graceful in accepting change?*

Taking unnecessary blame, causes feelings to spill over, hurting others around us. We wonder why life is so complex. Every girl struggles with negative thoughts about herself, but an abused girl's struggles are usually more severe.

Abuse comes in several ways. In earlier chapters I attempted to define sexual abuse. There are other mistreatments that damage the emotions as well, such as verbal and physical abuse. Adoption and divorce can also cause extreme insecurity.

Verbal abuse is if one is habitually tagged for wrong she didn't do, or if she is usual blame for trouble or spoken to in anger time after time.

Physical abuse is if one is hit with brutal harshness or thrown, or harm done to the body in other ways. Things like this cause tag-along feelings in the heart. Feelings of being devalued and unwanted. Verbal and physical abuse bear the lie of *rejection*, and keeps the truth of acceptance from the heart.

Perhaps we have no memories of being misused, but we still sense rejection from those we lived with. Having lived with a harsh, critical person makes it hard to trust anyone. It is hard to love when our parents didn't take time to love us and listen to what troubled us. We feel we will never be good enough to be of value to anyone, and question if God really cares.

Those who as a child have been given for adoption into another home will eventually come to a time of intense questioning. *Why did my real parents give me away?* The birth mother or birth father may have done the best they were able, wanting a good home for their child, but it still leaves her feeling deserted, wondering, *Wasn't I important enough to them? Why didn't they want me to be part of their life?* These agonizing questions cut deep into the wounded soul, and "abandoned" is written in the heart. Every child seeks love and security while growing up. Every child needs to belong. God understands and can reach out to that need.

Please remember that you were not born by accident. Your life has a purpose! Love never changes with God! He favors you and wants to write "*accepted*" in your heart.

In a divorce, you always wonder if you could have done something to persuade your parents to stay together, and you blame yourself for their separation. They may have told you the divorce wasn't because of you, but you still feel like a good-for-nothing because something else was more important to them. If your parents divorced each other, or your parents favored another child over you, you may feel you have "*worthless*" written across your heart.

In circumstances of this kind, people can get the feeling that unless they have the most important place in a game or the best place in class, they are of no value to anyone. These inferior feelings are not true. We need not be in first place to be loved and accepted by God. It is important to remember that God accepts us just the way we are.

Since the time sin entered the world, life is not perfect for anyone. While we live, sorrow resulting from the Fall cannot be avoided. But Christ has promised to walk with us through that sorrow and pain. We know that we can always find grace and mercy in time of need (Hebrews 4:16). We know that difficulties cannot separate us from God's love (Romans 8:35-39) and that He calls us His friend (John 15:15).

As hard as it is to imagine, even happy, loving families are imperfect. God spoke a special blessing when He said, "*Honor thy father and thy mother... that it may be well with thee*" (Ephesians 6:2a,3a). Maybe you wonder, *How can honoring my parents make things well for me?* When this direction from God is not followed something happens inside. Self respect is troubled. Hopeful wellbeing drops even further from the best intention, but respect adds strength to the day.

Parents are not perfect; no one but God is perfect. But God asks that we honor our parents, not speaking in disgust about them to others. When we speak respectfully to others of our parents and honor them, God will bless us.

Ways of thinking always become ways of behaving. When we think wrongly about ourselves, it causes us to act wrongly. Are we telling ourselves untruth?

To believe we are abandoned, rejected, or worthless is saying God made a mistake. God invites us to accept love from His Father heart into our own heart, turning from the lies of abandonment, rejection and worthlessness.

His invitation is always open, ready to set us free from wrong thoughts and actions.

Believing the truth of God's love and His acceptance opens the way for the music of heaven to flow through our heart. The Maker of our body and soul will send refreshing breezes of His grace. We can be in harmony with our Maker.

He that acknowledgeth the Son (Jesus)
hath the Father also (I John 2:23b).

In chapter eleven, "Right Thoughts," there is more about the lies we believe, and the truth that sets us free.

A Trampled Flower
can rise again

Prayer—

Dear Jesus, You see my heart. You see what is there. Why should I feel rejected when your arms are open wide to receive me? Teach me how to live clean and free. I want to walk with You. I give my life to You. I want to know your Father heart and your acceptance of me. I can't improve myself or make myself better; You love and accept me as I am. I want to love others with that same love. I ask, dear Lord, do your work in my heart. In Jesus' name, *Amen.*

In repentance and rest is your salvation, in quietness and trust is your strength (Isaiah 30:15 niv).

The LORD is righteous in all his ways and loving to all he has made.

The LORD is near to all who call on him, to all who call on him in truth.

He fulfills the desires of those who fear Him; he hears their cry and saves them (Psalm 145:17-19 niv).

The truth will set you free (John 8:32).

Activity—

Read Psalm 145

What are some great things this psalm speaks of?

A Trampled Flower can rise again

Abandoned
but Not Forsaken

Inside an adobe house in a land of green pastures and palm trees, Carmen blinked her sleepy eyes. Her older sister Rita was already walking into the kitchen.

Big sisters Estella and Lola were making breakfast. "Where is Mama?" Rita asked, stretching.

"I don't know," answered Lola. She was ten but big for her age. "Mama was gone when the sun awoke me this morning."

"Why does she go away with Omar," asked Carmen, following Rita into the kitchen? "Papa has gone too."

The older sisters knew the younger girls had a different papa than they did. Estella and Lola remembered when their dad had left to find another place to live. He went away because Mama was gone so often. They could remember when their own papa took them to the banana patch and gave them ripe bananas to eat.

"Omar doesn't want us girls to be along when he is with Mama," said Carmen dejectedly. Her lonely heart ached for Mama's smiles and her hugs. Why was Omar so very important to Mama? He always seemed very pleased when Mama left the girls by themselves and went down the road with him.

One night when Mama was putting baby Dolce in the hammock, Lola heard Omar say, "It's the girls or me. You need to decide. I don't want your girls in our life."

Thirteen-year-old Estella felt a yearning for Mother deep within her heart. "What shall the younger ones wear today?" she thought as she fumbled around to find clothes. Her sisters depended on her care for their needs.

After breakfast Rita and Carmen sat on the bed and played with baby Dolce. The morning sped on for the little ones. Lunchtime came, but Estella wasn't hungry. It was a terribly long day for the girls because Mama didn't come home until after dark.

Omar is bad. He is hurting us by taking away our mama. We need Mama! Carmen burst into tears as she dropped onto her bed that night. Lola stared into the darkness with troubled thoughts before she fell asleep. Three-year-old Dora lay quietly beside her.

What was wrong? Didn't Mama care about them? What had they done to make her leave them? Were they that bad? Why did she leave them and go away with Omar? The girls had no answers for their endless questions.

One afternoon a few weeks later, Rita and Carmen were playing under the big shade tree. "Let's pretend we're cooking like Mama does," said Rita.

"We'll have rice and cheese with tortillas," said Carmen. Little Dora sat contentedly, watching her sisters.

"Girls, Mama called us to come inside," said Estella, already walking into the house, carrying baby Dolce on her side. Inside, Lola was helping Mama put things in a bag.

"Estella, carry this bag of dresses," Mama said.

"Where are we going?" asked Carmen.

"We're going over the hill," answered Mama as she placed tortillas into a bag.

The sun shone on them as they climbed the hill. They were leaving town and heading toward the green countryside. Cows munched grass as the family passed them. A few sheep looked up curiously.

"Here is a place for you to rest," said Mama. "Sit here under the shade of this tree. It's too warm for you in the sun."

Some of the girls sat on the grass, while Rita and Carmen sat on a big rock. Mama walked down the road a ways and talked to some people. Soon an old truck stopped and Mama climbed into it.

After a long while Estella began thinking something was wrong. *What shall we do?* She wondered. The children waited for a long while and they were getting hungry. The yummy tortillas put a break into their long afternoon.

"Why doesn't Mama come back?" Carmen asked. No one knew the answer.

A car pulled off the road near them. Opening the door a man with a pleasant, kind expression walked over to them. "You have been here a long time, girls," he said. "Is somebody coming to pick you up here?"

"I don't know," said Estella, feeling responsible for her five sisters.

"You can come with me," the man said kindly. "We are very close to the Good Shepherd's Orphanage. It's getting dark. We'll find food and a place for you to sleep."

Carmen was glad to go somewhere, but her heart yearned for her mother.

Lola stared into the darkness. *Did Mama leave us and go to Omar? Did she bring us to this tree because she knew it was close to the orphanage?*

"My name is Jacob," said the man gently, picking up one of their bags. "We are your friends." The girls picked up the rest of their bags, and followed the man. Rita and Carmen held each other's hands.

The younger girls sensed what the older ones already knew—their mama had left them there so someone would find them and care for them. *Where was she now? Would they ever see her again? Didn't she care where they were? Why not?*

Carmen sobbed on Rita's shoulder. Rita hurt so much inside she felt like she would break. *Why did Omar take our mama away?*

Their new friends at the orphanage found homes for each of the girls. Estella and Lola went to live at Dale and Ruth's house, while Rita and Carmen lived at Mark and Rachel's house. Sam and Carla took baby Dolce with them. Sweet little Dora went to the orphanage with Mama Juanita.

Dolce and Dora didn't find the same turmoil inside their older sisters felt. Estella and Lola were torn and confused. Dale and Ruth often told them how much God loves them. Friends at school and church talked kindly to them. The girls had never experienced such love from people, and it felt wonderful and scary at the same time. But no matter how others loved them, they always wondered where their mama and papa were.

After some weeks, Lola said to Estella, "Surely our papa would love us. Surely he has a lot of money and would give us a lot of things. Come with me and let's go find him."

The next day they wrote a note to Dale and Ruth. It said, "We went to look for our papa."

The girls searched for several days. When they found him, he was drunk, lying in the street. Disappointment broke their hearts. They had

hoped he'd care about them, but now their dream was dashed.

Two women on a park bench noticed the sad sisters. "He'll be all right tomorrow," said one of the women carelessly, trying to make them feel better.

The girls hurried away.

Lola noticed some girls laughing nearby. *They are so happy*, she thought. *Maybe I could be happy too if I had someone to really love and care about me.* Lola cried bitterly into her hands. "Where shall we go now? What can we do?"

The sisters decided to go back to Dale and Ruth's house. They found that Dale and Ruth loved them as much as before. Estella felt their love and eventually accepted Christ into her heart and slowly learned to trust God and His love for her.

But Lola's heart was torn and bitter. *If I could live somewhere else, I'd be much happier,* she thought. She told Estella she wanted new friends. Upon that decision, she left the protection of Dale and Ruth's Christian home to find people she thought were friends. She thought people were happy if they could laugh and make a lot of noise. But she soon discovered happiness like that was like a bubble which burst quickly. Lola still sought release for the deep pain she felt. God still loves her and longs for her to come to Him. When she is hungry for true answers, God will show her the way to Him.

Later Estella married a good Christian man, but she never forgot the rejection she felt when she was young. She saw children happily reaching to touch their papa's face, and when he smiled back she desperately wanted such love for her children. She hadn't experienced that love when she was a child, but she knew God could make it possible for her family.

She pondered Jesus' sweet love for her. "I will never leave you; I will always care for you." She would trust Him. Thinking honestly about her sad heart, she prayed, "Lord, I want to look on Your dear face. Your love will help me be the mother you want me to be. And thank you for a Christian husband, a good papa for our children."

Prayer drew her into the presence of Jesus. Estella knew that Jesus wanted to put the broken

pieces of her heart together. He would help her be the loving mother that she wanted for her child.

After their mother abandoned the girls, Rita and Carmen lived with friends until Rita was fourteen. On her birthday the two girls moved into Light and Hope Orphanage. The girls felt comfortable with Mama Juanita's smiles and warm love.

Dora had already been with Mama Juanita for two years. She was only four when mama left and had easily adapted to life in the orphanage.

Rita found it hard to become part of the fun. Dark hair fell around her sad eyes as she moved about in her quiet manner. Dear Mama Juanita tried to reach that lonely spot in her aching heart.

There was always some game or action going to bring the home to life. Sometimes Carmen helped play with the children, but mostly she clung to Rita. Rita wondered why she felt so very much alone, even while she was in the home with Mama Juanita and her sisters.

"Rita, is something troubling you?" Mama Juanita would ask, putting her arm around her.

"I don't know," Rita would answer. She didn't understand that she was bitter because her mother had abandoned her and her sisters. She couldn't make herself be part of the activities. She felt locked in a lonely room of worthlessness. *If Mama didn't love me, how can anyone else love me?* she thought.

Mama Juanita saw her sad heart. "My dear girl, I love you. And even more, Jesus loves you and understands the pain you feel. He can touch sad hearts. Jesus' love reaches through the darkest places." God was so gracious to bring these precious girls into her life. What suffering these young and tender hearts must feel.

In the quiet evening Carmen found Rita, "Just think, if Omar hadn't come and taken Mama away we could still have her," she shared.

Bitterness had taken root in the girls hearts, and there was fear of being rejected again. But God wanted to show the girls His love.

A Trampled Flower can rise again

Neighbors John and Amanda had given the orphanage a basket of tomatoes. "We want to walk over and thank John and Amanda for their gift of tomatoes they gave yesterday," said Mama Juanita. The girls put on their sandals and followed her through the doorway. They walked past the pineapples and down the dusty road.

"Hello, Amanda," said Juanita. "How are you today?" Amy and Anna were helping their mother wash clothes. They left Amanda's side to play with Rita and Carmen.

"I like to help Mama and make soap bubbles on the clothing," said Amy.

"Sometimes it looks like a mountain with snow," said Anna, laughing.

Something hit Rita's heart. What was it? Her desire for Mama and the fun they had at Mama's house grew in her mind and abandonment filled her sad, aching heart again. Reminiscing was too painful for her. Tears stung her eyes, but she quickly wiped them away. "No one may see me cry," she reasoned.

"Come see our new pineapple patch," said Anna. "Papa just planted them last evening."

Rita walked down the path after the other girls. Mama felt so far away. *Where is Mama now?* she wondered. *Where is my papa?* Rita's thoughts became a mass of churning confusion. She tried to shut off the pain. It wouldn't hurt as much if she didn't let it be real.

Juanita and Amanda talked of the good things God was doing for them. "Thanks for the tomatoes you sent over yesterday. The children really enjoyed the chili and rice we made with them," said Juanita, as the girls came around the corner of the house. "It's time we start home. Are you ready, girls?"

Rita and Carmen said good-bye, and started up the road with Mama Juanita.

Mama Juanita exclaimed, "What a beautiful blue sky God made for all to see. Everybody from the east to the west can know God's great love. He shows us in things like those big, fluffy white clouds in the sky! Like the sky, His love has no end."

Rita didn't want to hear about God and she didn't want to open her heart to people. It hurt too badly to be real. It was less painful to shut

people out of her life. It felt better to be alone in an empty room of her heart and close the door.

Mama Juanita noticed Rita's painful silence and put her arm around her. "God's love is like a circle," she told her. "It never ends. It's around and around you. He knows the struggle in your heart, and understands what you want before you pray. That's how much God loves you."

Rita tried to think how such love would feel. She hoped that sometime she could find that love.

Rita and Carmen were both well-behaved girls. Slowly, slowly they felt love reaching into their deep hurts. Slowly, slowly the light was coming into their dark, lonely hearts. In stories they heard of Jesus' love while He lived here on earth. They could see God's love in the hearts of the caregivers.

At sixteen Rita accepted Jesus as her Saviour and knew Him to be her constant Friend. Sometimes she still suffered dejection and felt it was easier to sit in a corner alone, while others seemed to have a good time.

Then Rita would often pray, "Jesus, please help me to be free in your love." She would get up and try to show love to others. She felt better that way.

A few years later Carmen also accepted Jesus into her heart. Jesus was now their faithful companion through life. It wasn't always easy, but He brought a love-light into their hearts, and it helped in lonely times to know He cared for them.

Rita still longed to see her mother. *Maybe if I could talk to her, I could overcome my struggle with bitterness,* she thought.

Later their mother came to visit them. While talking with her mother, Rita discovered her Mother was trying to cover pain in her own life. She found out that Mama's own life was very empty. She was trying to fill it with fun things in this world. *Poor Mama, Jesus could help her too.* More visits with her poor suffering mother helped Rita get rid of some of her bitter feelings.

Rita's mother brought two more little sisters to the orphanage. Omar didn't have time for children. *Poor Mama, what pain she must feel.*

Sometimes Mama Juanita would take the girls along with her on a trip. A visa made this possible. But that was used so often, it expired. Mama Juanita had expenses to pay and she had to get another job to pay for these needs. She had to leave the girls for several months.

Friends of the orphanage built a house for Rita and Carmen. Estella's happy home was close by. Rita and Carmen were now twenty-one and eighteen years old.

Rita would talk with Mama Juanita on the telephone. "All is well," she said, "but Carmen has left to live with a man. "

"I am very sorry to hear that," said Mama Juanita. "I will pray that God will help Carmen not to forget His love."

Carmen was not happy. How could she be? She would panic about the future. She feared being alone. She looked for love to fill the painful void. *Where is love? It's more than making love with a man. Ralph doesn't understand how I need love.* Hope was dangling on a thread. It looked like more disappointment lay ahead.

Carmen numbly folded the sun-dried shirt. *I can't do this any longer,* she said to herself. *Ralph has skipped out and spent half a day with Sue instead of working in the field. Last week I didn't know where he was for two days. And last night, I don't know why he wasn't home till near morning. Is life going to always be trouble?* Betrayal held her in pangs of bitterness.

Carmen came back to live with Rita. Her wrong choices had brought much pain into her troubled life. She found refuge in her heavenly Father. His arms of love circled around her aching heart again. She knew His love was far better than anything the world had to offer.

A little girl was born to Carmen, and she is now teaching her the wonderful truth of Jesus. Many times when she is lonely, she looks to Jesus in prayer. "I love You, Lord, because You are here with me and understand my heart. I love You because You took me in when I was so undeserving. I love You because You never change. You know the great task I have in teaching Elizabeth. It looks so big to me, but I know I am not alone, even if I feel alone, because You are always with me. Thank you, Jesus, Amen."

While they had taken trips with Mama Juanita, a young Christian man named Mark had come to know Rita. He wanted to be friends with her, and traveled to visit her. Mark lived at Dale and Ruth's house and walked with Rita to church. A few weeks later he returned to his distant home, but came back months later to visit Rita again.

A year later, Mark and Rita were married. Their Christian home was a happy home. God blessed them with children. Sometimes Rita struggled with fears. *What if Mark doesn't really love me? she thought.* Dark shadows filled her lonely heart. *How can I be of any worth?* She searched for assurance, but found only emptiness. *How can I be a good mother?* she asked herself again.

"You can't be a good mother," echoed off the walls of fear.

She was scared, and began to cry to God in prayer, "I can't, Lord. I can't be a good mother without You. Help me, Lord, to show Your love to my dear children. Your love to me is so deep, it's so wide, it's so real, and it's so strong."

Comfort of the Lord's presence again filled her heart. Her children were happily playing on the floor. *God wants our simple trust,* she mused. *I am His child. The joy of the Lord is my strength.*

Questions—

1. Was Rita free of conflict after she became a Christian or had a family of her own?

2. Why does God allow tests to come into our life?

Chapter Six
God's Heart for Relationship

*The sea is his, and he made it: And
his hands formed the dry land. ...For
he is our God; and we are the people
of his pasture (Psalm 95:5,7a).*

If God said "It is good,"
Then why is there pain?

There once was a garden in an eastern
wonderland. All things in this pleasant land were
only good and perfect. There were trees of every
kind and luscious fruit grew unblemished. A clear
river of excellent water parted into four, to sustain
the garden's beauty. A mist went up and watered
every plant. No sin had entered this peaceful
place where God walked and talked with man.

There was fruit to eat of any tree to their liking—all but one of which God said not to eat.

We wonder what life was like in the Garden of Eden. It as a place of absolute contentment—a place where God met with sinless man and woman, and they had fellowship.

There was not a hint of selfish inclination, not a nudge of pain, till Satan as a serpent slipped into the tree they were told not to eat of. Slyly he spoke his words of deception, "God wants to keep something good from you; it is pleasant to the eyes and will make you wise as God."

"It looks good for food," reasoned Eve listening to the serpent. She reached out, picked some of the fruit, and ate. The man also partook. God was with them in the garden, but they didn't turn to Him for help. Now they were afraid because they had disobeyed God, and they wanted to hide. God said they both must leave the garden, never to enter again. Thereafter man was born with sin. But God provided the way back to Himself.

God's greatest longing is for fellowship with mankind.

A Trampled Flower
can rise again

God promised a Saviour to destroy the power of sin. He would dwell in any man or woman who chose to accept Him into his or her heart.

Will we give ourselves to that love He extends to us today?

His care for us is obvious: this Great God knows our thoughts and even the number of hairs on our head. He knows the future as well as the past.

Since the beginning, from Creation, there are marvels preserved for our joyful attention. We can see them every day.

An artist cannot capture the thrill of sunset's awesome colors. God alone paints the hue that scopes the western skies.

Trees make a home for birds that twitter and sing and build nests for their young. Slopes bloom in colorful array, giving home to animals that are furry and reptiles that aren't so furry. God knows the place of every living thing!

On lofty heights glaciers melt into streams, and the thunder of waterfalls sounds through the air. Quiet streams flow from the forest shade like sparkling ribbons. Fish swim rapidly after their prey or tag along lazily in deep lakes.

God made all of this by merely speaking a word! Stars and galaxies declare His greatness!

Somebody is running the universe!

God made the earth a beautiful place for us to call home. But there is something even better than observing the creation, and that is to know our Creator.

When many difficult questions churn in our mind, His constant care and awesome handiwork seem harder to notice. Questions come, like.....

This world is so beautiful, why did sin come to ruin it?

Why do children suffer?

Why do moms and dads leave their children?

Why is there so much sadness in my world?

Why do men do sinful things if God made everything good?

Why do women do sinful things if God made everything good?

Through disobedience, all men and women's hearts became sinful. Now selfish hearts think only of themselves. A selfish person doesn't want to consider how he or she has hurt another.

Because of sexual abuse a girl may feel ugly about herself and say, "I was born only to suffer pain. There is nothing else in life for me."

Life in this fallen world has many disappointments, but you were not made to suffer agonizing emotional pain. Jesus understands your struggles. He sees everything—when you sit down and when you stand up. Read Psalm 139:2.

God the Father heard Jesus pray for you and will grant the request of His beloved Son.

I pray not for the world, but for them which thou hast given me; for they are thine (John 17:9).
...keep them from the evil (John 17:15b).

By faith we know His assuring presence. Sin cannot molest us there. We can find that place of rest near to the heart of God.

Can a girl who was abused ever believe that God's plan for sex is beautiful and good? Yes! It is possible through knowing God's love.

Our girls stayed at home with our friends' children while my husband and I went with them to a park, where picnic tables were scattered under a spread of trees. We sat together at a table under the shade that day in early May. My friend had her pencil in hand with paper alongside. I began sharing the long, hidden pain of my heart, telling it all, giving details of places and times and the ruin I had felt... how vulnerable I was to let someone conspire against me... the apathy I faced... the defeat and loneliness.... how hopeless it looked to ever be normal again. I told of the tears and sorrow of the present day struggles, the grief I have of my own teen years when I see the joy my girls have in sharing with other girls. All morning I shared incidents of loneliness and pain.

When I was done; my friend numbered fourteen points of pain and passed the paper to me to read. Slowly I read the points—they described me well—then I passed it back to her, my heart yearning for rest. "That is me," I said.

The four of us then prayed together over each point, one at a time. First my husband prayed that I could open my heart to that hurt. Then I prayed, opening my heart, pouring out all the pain and despair before the Lord, asking Him to come into its place. Then my friend's husband prayed that I be blessed by God's presence in that place, and be led in His goodness. Going over each of the fourteen points, one at a time in prayer, made them no longer mine.

When we returned home, I was weary from all I had put into sharing, but there was tranquility in my new journey.

God made everything good. Even if people use sex in a wrong way, God's plan is good. It is good only with one man and one woman who are married to each other (Mark 10: 6-9).

The hands of God molded and shaped the first man from the dust of the ground. He breathed into him and Adam became a living soul. He formed Eve while Adam was resting and she became a living soul. It is awesome to believe how very close we are to the God who created us.

God holds the beginning of life in His hands as it develops in the mother's uterus. When a baby's form begins, there is life with a valuable eternal soul. The world seeks to abort babies, but God touches the embryo, and a new life is formed. In its very start, the heartbeat of the embryo is begun by God. Babies are precious because they reflect His image. The embryo is protected in the womb by God's good plan.

God is Mercy and Goodness. He gives Hope!

God is Faithful, He is Love, and knows your heart!

He is Kindness and cares deeply for you!

God has a plan for all who seek His way.

There is a God-shaped vacuum in the heart that will be satisfied with none other than God Himself. We cannot make our heart good. We all need God to do the changing.

God has shown His love to man, the crowning part of His creation. He gave heaven's best, the sacrifice of love, to woo us from sin.

No person can ever explain God's great heart of love. But by acknowledging our sin, accepting His love, and inviting Jesus into our heart, our whole life can be changed.

He is perfecting holiness in those who walk with Him (II Corinthians 7:1).

God is our Refuge –
when things around us become difficult.

God is our Tower of Strength –
when we know our weakness.

God is our understanding Father –
when confusion seems to surround us.

Read aloud:
So God created man in his own image, in the image of God created he him; male and female created he them… God saw everything that he had made, and behold, it was very good (Genesis 1:27,31).

Prayer—

Dear Jesus, Your love for me is more than I can comprehend. It is like a fountain that keeps running over onto me. In Your tender care You know all the thoughts of my heart. You see when a little sparrow falls to the ground. How much more you care about me. Help me to give to you everything that I am. I want to trust my future to you as my wise Father, as One who wants the best for me. In Jesus' name, *Amen*.

Our Father which art in heaven,

Hallowed be Thy name,

Thy kingdom come,

Thy will be done

On earth as it is in heaven.

Give us this day our daily bread,

And forgive us our debts

As we forgive our debtors.

And lead us not into temptation

But deliver us from evil.

For Thine is the kingdom,

And the power,

And the glory,

Forever.

Amen.

Activity—

Take a walk outdoors to gaze upon the handiwork of our great God.

1. Look up. Can you see the end of space? What is beyond what you can see? Psalm 33:6 tells us God made all the host of heaven by the breath of His mouth.

2. What lies between you and the horizons? What is beyond them? What does all this tell us about God?

Sylvia Makes a Choice

Sylvia scanned the table of stacked romance novels at the garage sale. On each cover a handsome man stood near a beautiful woman, looking adoringly up at him. The books were only 25 cents each.

"Hey, let's buy some," her friend suggested. "We can read them, then share them. I just love these books."

Sylvia bought several. She took them home and hid them in a special place. Mother would certainly object to books with such covers. As she pored over the pages, Sylvia was thrilled with the excitement of love, imagining men adoring her, pursuing her, and chasing her. She wanted so much to fall in love, to be adored.

Yet deep down in she knew Aunt Thelma wouldn't approve either, or let her daughters spend time reading romance novels.

What is it like to be in real love anyway? Sylvia wondered.

One evening while visiting with her cousins, Aunt Thelma shared with fifteen-year-old Sylvia what it is like to be a woman and about being in love. She encouraged Sylvia to stop reading the romance novels because they distract from what true love is.

"Novels will take your thoughts and feelings to places with little reserve," she told her. "Instead of reading books like that, I'd like to encourage you to read the Bible and other books that draw you nearer to God. Seek to be pure, and pursue courtship only with a godly marriage as a goal."

"Courtship is a special friendship between a boy and a girl who want to marry," continued Aunt Thelma. "They get to know each other and share their life goals. Courtship is a time for learning to know each other's personality, as well as likes and dislikes, and dreams and pursuits. It is not a time to know what feels good to each other's body or set loose a roller coaster of emotions."

Sylvia knew there were two paths from which she could choose: a path of freedom and light, or a path of deception and darkness. She saw the beauty in following God's design for purity and giving a respectful place to a young man in a special friendship.

For several weeks she pondered these thoughts, then she got rid of the novels. She would keep herself pure, she decided. She would refrain from close intimacy. She would choose to not sit tight for hugs and selfish lust. Her mother told her it would save her a lot of trouble. Aunt Thelma was right.

A few weeks after Sylvia's sixteenth birthday, she sat shyly in a large youth group eating dinner at Kate's Kitchen and Open Grill. *So many young people and I know only a few! It looks like everyone is enjoying it more than I am.*

When they were finished eating, a friendly girl walked up to her. "Hi, my name's Beulah. Let's go outside on the lawn.

"I work here at Kate's. We do catering too," Beulah went on. "Sometimes we are very busy, but not always. I like working with everyone here. There are enough of us working that we can easily ask for days off."

Sylvia noticed Beulah seemed at ease with people and knew what to say and do in any given situation. She seemed like a friend to everyone.

When they were alone, Beulah shared her loneliness with Sylvia. "All my brothers and sisters are married. Last summer my best friends moved away to northern Alberta, and I really miss them. But I'm glad I have you for my friend."

The next weekend, Sylvia was with the youth for a chorus program. Beulah smiled as she walked in and sat beside Sylvia. "I'm glad you're my special friend," she whispered. "Life isn't as lonely when you have a friend." Sylvia smiled shyly in response. It warmed her heart to feel Beulah's acceptance of her.

Later that evening, Beulah shared stories of painful times growing up. Her family had lived in a poor section of town. Her father was killed when his truck went over an embankment on a foggy night. After his death the family struggled even harder financially.

Sylvia felt a sense of security to have a friend older and wiser but still willing to confide in her. She saw that Beulah felt a lot of pain, and because Sylvia wanted to be helpful she was glad to support Beulah.

The next Saturday afternoon Beulah stopped at Sylvia's home. "Come to my house, and we can go to church together in the morning. After the meeting you can have lunch at my house, and we can have the afternoon together."

"Sure, I'll come with you," Sylvia answered. She felt a little guilty when she thought of her cousins and Aunt Thelma. They had been good friends, but now she didn't feel so close to them because she spent more of her time with Beulah. She wondered if they were feeling left out.

That night at her place, Beulah read the Bible to Sylvia followed by prayer aloud. Again she shared sad stories of her life. Sylvia admired Beulah's openness about spiritual things and pitied her for the many difficulties she had had in her life. She wanted to help Beulah in her sadness.

Before going to sleep, Beulah took Sylvia's hand and snuggled close to her. A strange, excited feeling came over Sylvia. Then Beulah hugged her warmly. *What does this mean?* Sylvia felt confused. Beulah put her hands on Sylvia's breasts, stroking and patting her, giving her more hugs. Sylvia felt both excited and trapped.

The girls spent more weekends together. There were intimate places they did not touch, but still it seemed wrong to share as much as they did. Sylvia felt alone, wondering if she should tell someone what Beulah did to her, but feeling too embarrassed to talk about it.

In the next weeks and months, Beulah sometimes asked Sylvia to go along when Kate's Kitchen and Open Grill catered a meal. The girls spent many weekends together away from home. Sylvia's mother seemed to think Beulah was a good friend for her daughter, though Beulah seldom came to Sylvia's house.

The girls seemed to be good friends for over a year, but because of the way they privately handled each other's bodies, Sylvia doubted their friendship was as good and right as it appeared. Feeling sexually pursued and aroused by Beulah, and herself drawn to it, made Sylvia feel removed from the rest of life around her. She felt numb to happiness or sadness.

One day when Beulah asked Sylvia to come home with her again, Sylvia asked, "Shouldn't we tell someone about what we do with each other when we are alone? Maybe someone can help us stop doing it?" But Beulah only stared straight ahead without saying a word.

As time went on, the girls gave each other many cards and gifts, but Sylvia still felt lonely. When she thought of her cousins she felt sick, forgotten and locked in a world all alone. Sylvia became very quiet and seldom spoke when people were around her. Besides, she didn't need to talk because she was often with Beulah and Beulah talked freely to everyone. No one knew Sylvia's inner pain, and she didn't tell anyone about it either. Life became routine, without a change. Sylvia felt like a robot, moving like a machine through her day.

During those lonely years, sometimes hope visited her heart. *Maybe I could talk with someone about my questions and guilt. Should I talk with Aunt Thelma or a psychiatrist?*

Will I ever feel smiles and tears like other people do? Will I ever be able to talk freely with my cousins again?

Words from an old hymn held Sylvia's mind, and gave her comfort and a sense of hope. *Maybe things could be different sometime. Maybe it's true that God will give victory over wrong, no matter how strong. But how can I find God?*

One day Aunt Thelma invited Sylvia to a prayer meeting at her house. A few families gathered and sat in the large living room that was set up for the occasion. One of the brethren shared his heart. "Do you long for peace? Does sin have a hold on you? Jesus died to cleanse us from sin and He arose from the dead to give power to a new life. Believe in His name and He will set you free."

Light of hope began to show through Sylvia's darkness.

Later, when she was alone she asked God to do His saving work in her heart. God answered her prayer, she knew. The next Sunday she went to church with her cousins; the crowd was so big she felt timid even when the girls included her in their activities. Aunt Thelma was glad to have Sylvia come to church. She knew Sylvia found peace because her countenance had changed to being joyful, and she took to Christian friends. But Sylvia never shared the story of her relationship with Beulah.

That weekend Sylvia told Beulah about the new life she had found in Jesus. "That's fine," Beulah said. "You can come to my house anyway."

"But it's going to be different now," Sylvia said. And it was! Sylvia constantly clung to the treasure of her new joy in Christ's love. She refused to return to the sexual pleasures she used to indulge in with Beulah.

Sylvia moved along in her life with new friends. When she could, she shared about the joy and peace God had given her. While she was glad for new friends, she struggled deeply as to whether she deserved their love. It felt good to be with her cousins again after having mostly ignored them for several years, but something still seemed to distract her freedom.

When she occasionally met Beulah, Sylvia felt no hatred for her and talked respectfully to her.

The pain of her abuse held onto Sylvia. Aunt Thelma noticed her stress and insecurity. One afternoon Aunt Thelma's caring heart moved Sylvia to tell her everything about those wasted years.

Aunt Thelma and Sylvia prayed together, opening the door of pain to the Saviour for healing. She found rejection no longer ruled her. Her Saviour had become her understanding Friend.

Sylvia came to know that she could trust God to plan her days, to keep her in difficult times. She could share His love with those around her. Now, instead of negative thoughts about herself, she knows God treasures her. He gave her a new way to live.

She found the answer she had wanted for so long. The Great Physician, Jesus, understood pain, and had come to heal her heart and life.

When grief merges into our present;

Open the door to look at pain.

Where did it begin?

Where has it taken you?

Freedom is the fruit of honesty.

Questions—

1. How long can pain be covered until it goes away?

2. How can you invite healing?

Chapter Seven
Choice That Counts

"For I know the thoughts that I think toward you," says the Lord, "thoughts of peace and not of evil, to give you a future and a hope" (Jeremiah 29:11 nkjv).

Choice Brings Results With It

If someone has a valuable gift or piece of money, it is not put on display but is shown only to someone special. If it were set out for display, it might someday be missing, or it may be tarnished if too many people touch it.

Modesty is opposed to extreme boldness. A Godly woman wants to reflect the glory of God and not to draw attention to herself. Dressing modestly is a way of hiding the treasure God gave her, and keeping it safe and special. A girl who is discreet or discerning shows respect to herself and those she meets. Decent men are not ashamed to look upon her. Her attire shuns intoxicated passion, but instead displays the beautiful flower of chastity.

God created Adam and Eve in His own image and likeness. There is more in this than I can define, but the first man and woman were perfect and beautiful. The Bible points out that they were naked and not ashamed of it. But after sin, they became ashamed and didn't want to be seen without clothes. Finding fig leaves, they sewed them together to cover themselves. That didn't cover them well enough so the LORD clothed them with animal skins (Genesis 3:21).

Satan spoiled God's good plan for men and women's bodies, and he still wants to spoil God's good plan today.

Wearing fewer clothes or tight clothes to reveal the bosom and hip draws attention to the girl, not to the One who created her. He made these curves to be attractive and beautiful, but not to be flaunted and shown off.

When a girl dresses modestly, she shows respect to herself and others. She is reminded that God designed her body for a good purpose. It is so beautiful and special; its purity is to be treasured.

Modesty affects more than just clothes. It also concerns the way she talks and moves her body. Sometimes young women are seen acting in certain ways to be noticed. They walk with an extra twist, or cock their head and move their eyes to get attention from men. Christian women can help make it possible for men to stay pure, not only in their bodies, but also in their minds.

Modesty in clothes as well as actions will affect the rest of her life, as well as encourage others' lives.

I found a new way of living that day at the park. The Lord was now my Saviour and Friend, my Helper and Counselor, my Shepherd and Guide. My life became an open walk of prayer.

Sometimes I want to reject the pain I feel from being misunderstood. I tussle with this pain while Jesus is waiting with open arms to take this wearisome care for me. I look up and find Him a Friend who listens, a Counselor who teaches, and a Guide who leads the way.

One way I found Him was to allow myself to become as nothing at the feet of Jesus—to expose everything. Still believing in God's love for me, I saw as in a vision nail-scarred hands, and I said in surprise, "Jesus, You are here!"

And He answered, "Yes, I was also misunderstood and suffered pain, dying on the cross to give everything for you. You are never alone. I am always with you no matter what your difficulty."

Such a Friend! I want to always walk with Him.

God has given inborn wisdom called intuition. It makes us aware deep inside whether a person is to be trusted or not. It senses when our purity has been threatened or violated by remarks or gestures given our way. Intuition is God's way of directing us out of danger.

A girl may have already accepted Christ in her heart. She wants her life to be in service for her Lord. But why, she wonders, hasn't that choice made life easier?

We are on a battlefield in enemy territory. Satan is the enemy and he hates everyone. His goal is to destroy any effort for good. As the enemy of God, he makes sin appear attractive when it is actually destructive, and he makes the good things seem impossible to achieve. We can choose, however, to not follow his invitation to sin. The choice we make will always have results, and the results affect more people than just you.

Sometimes a girl finds it hard to accept herself the way God made her, either in her body or her personality. While she may wish to be like someone else she admires, she must realize that God made her for a specific purpose and a plan of His own.

There are quiet, observant people who rarely share deep thoughts. Others express their ideas more freely. When each one considers what another contributes to a relationship, each personality can be good and useful. Personality and good choices can bless and encourage others even when one is not aware of it.

The truth is that God made each one of us special in His unique plan. God designed everyone with the ability and potential to offer beauty to relationships.

Jesus is the WAY, flooding your path with light and leading you on.

Jesus is the TRUTH; believing truth gives you freedom to live!

Jesus is LIFE, giving power to live victoriously over self and sin.

And they shall be mine, saith the Lord of hosts, In that day when I make up my jewels (Malachi 3:17a).

Think how carefully an artist works on his project. God does much more for you. He doesn't slumber or sleep, but tirelessly, carefully works in you, shaping your life for His purpose. His plan is to design His beauty in you.

Prayer–

"Lord Jesus, I praise You for every good thing done in my life. I want others to think more about You and Your goodness than about me. Keep me from falling into selfish thinking. In Your good plan, help me to be a blessing and an encouragement to others. Help me to make right choices that would please You. I want to show Your love to others. Help all who are sad and abused to find Your rich love. Bring hope to their hearts. In Jesus' name, *Amen*.

Activity—

Write Malachi 3:17a on a long, narrow piece of paper and keep it for a book marker.

Chapter Eight
The Miracle of a Seed

Except a corn of wheat fall into the ground and die, it abideth alone: but if it die, it bringeth forth much fruit (John 12:24).

Encouragement to Purpose and Change

One day the girls put a vase of flowers on a corner stand where many pass by. I mentioned they could easily get knocked down if left there, but the girls thought they looked so lovely on the stand.

Later, the lovely vase of roses was knocked to the floor. Ordinarily, I would have scolded them accusingly, but this time I said nothing. I marveled at the work of God's grace in my heart.

The trust of relationship felt strange to us, but the long journey of healing had begun.

The hiding place in Christ offers me not only a rest that loves, but also a love that rests. God wants me to rest in Him. I found it good for me to remain quiet and let God touch hearts.

As I pondered other relationships, God brought light to me in other circumstances as well. I saw that none of us are sufficient of ourselves; but our sufficiency is of God. Our need of God is mutual.

This illuminated my path. I no longer verbally beat myself and others for shortcomings and failures. God wants to take the "hard to understand" things and make something beautiful with them. He is still doing that for me.

God wants our focus and trust. He surely will be there for all our today's and tomorrows.

A delicate daisy of pastel color begins as a very small seed. Soil covers the seed and after several days a tiny sprout surfaces to light. With sun, water, and loving care, the new seedling brings forth green leaves. Buds open revealing shades of beautiful lavender, white, pink or yellow. Everyone enjoys a vase of daisies on the table in the warm days of summer.

Being painfully honest about emotional pain is like putting a seed into the ground to die. Sorrow softens the soil of the heart, making it possible for good seed to grow. It feels like death now, but with honest commitment we reap better things.

Healing continues through pain and sorrow. Trying to avoid sorrow can delay our quest for healing.

God bestows strength to live noble and right. It can be that in joy we find strength and assurance, or in tears we find strength and courage in a given need.

With Jesus given first place in the heart, one is never alone in this journey.

We may ask questions. What is it like to have victory over sin? How can the image of Christ reflect in my heart? How does it work? Is it happening when I feel so wrong inside?

Doubts may assail... *Can I hope of ever becoming a beautiful, graceful woman? I'm afraid to expose who I really am? I'm young and have a long life ahead of me.*

God sees and understands the hesitancy to draw near to Him. It was spoken of Jesus; *A bruised reed He will not break, and a smoking flax He will not quench: He shall bring forth judgement in truth.* These words taken from Isaiah 43:3 and Matthew 12:20 are changed to make it clearer. He judges truthfully in mercy.

The Bible gives a pattern of how to think. When our thoughts change, the rest of our life changes too.

"Finally, [girls] whatsoever things are true, whatsoever things are honest, whatsoever things are just, whatsoever things are pure, whatsoever things are lovely, whatsoever things are of good report, and if there be any virtue, and if there be any praise, think on these things." Philippians 4:8

A Trampled Flower
can rise again

Press forward! Our Captain Jesus arose from the dead to give us victory and freedom. Christian warfare is part of our walk on earth. In God's care a tiny seedling breaks through stone and pavement to sunlight. How remarkable!

Fire and heat refine gold to a pure and clean shimmer reflecting an image. So also God plans difficult times, opening windows of heaven with fair flowers of virtue – good conduct, honesty, purity and fairness. In this way His image can reflect in our heart. That is beautiful!

"And he shall sit as a refiner, and purge them as gold and silver that they may offer unto the LORD an offering of righteousness." Malachi 3:3

No matter how hard life may be, He can strengthen your heart and mind to make right choices and you can grow tall and beautiful in the flower of womanhood.

God's passion is to bless every growing daughter of the King. His nature is undying love to fulfill His purpose in you, the person of His creation.

Prayer–

"Dear Lord Jesus, thank You for Your great love to me. You know everything about my life, my past, present and future. I want to be honest with You about every part of my life. I have needs, (tell Him your needs,) but You are greater than my needs. You are the Healer of my hurts, (tell Him your hurts). Help me to stay pure. Help me bring praise and glory to Your name. Make me wise to know what true love is. You are my refuge, and You can keep me from evil. In Jesus' name, *Amen*.

A Trampled Flower
can rise again

"If ye have faith as a grain of mustard seed… nothing shall be impossible unto you." (Matthew 17:20) Faith can remove mountains.

"He that goeth forth and weepeth, bearing precious seed, shall doubtless come again with rejoicing, bringing his sheaves with him." (Psalm 126:6)

Activity—

Gather a bouquet of flowers for a vase.

Jesus the Son

Giving strong opinions to boost my weakness

Loosing Self Control

No Satisfied Answers

Talking unkindly about others

Fearful Angry Words

Hating Myself Bad Names

Lonely Hurting Others

Confusion

Feeling Worthless

Believing lies about yourself

Fear & Anger

Where are my friends?

...*A Light* that shineth in a dark place, until the day dawn, and the day star arise in your hearts.
II Peter 1:19

Fearful "I Can't" Shadows

Hatred

Abuse-Pain

Doubts-Fear

Selfishness

Anger

Rejection

Chapter Nine
Believing Lies Withers a Flower

Control of Lies and the Outcome

There are times in our life that we feel like a drooping flower. Clouds have covered the sun. It feels like light, love, and gladness are all gone from the heart.

Sometimes a flower droops because the enemy's lies are eating away at the root. Are we processing lies from the root of rejection?

When harmful lies are at the root of the flower, and not given in trust to Jesus, fruits of its kind grow up in the heart. Feeling of little worth and hopeless causes good intentions to droop.

Drooping Leaves
Feeling worthless

Think about what shows up in our character when we feel worthless. Can we accept love from God? Is it easy to accept love from others when we feel as if we have no value or beauty?

Maybe we don't feel worthy of anyone's love. When we can't accept love in our heart, there is no love there to give away. How can the withered leaf of rejection be revived?

In His mercy God accepts us as we are. He offers genuine, free love, waiting for our taking. Believing His acceptance will pour grace into the trusting heart and allow it to flow out to others.

Is my heart empty enough so God can fill it? Is it selfless enough so God can direct it? A splash of courage will refresh this withered leaf.

Anger

Usually when we are hurt by someone, we feel angry inside. We can feel a quiet, sullen anger, or an anger that can be heard and felt by others. It can be feeling angry with God for allowing disappointments to happen. Remember God is not the source of harm.

> *God is light, and in him is no darkness at all (1 John 1:5b).*

Anger that spills suddenly and repeatedly, followed by regret, can be the result of a controlling fear that envelops an abused girl. A girl can be angry with herself because she thinks, *I should have known better than to do that. It was entirely my fault.* When she is hard on herself, she also becomes harsh with others, and that makes the leaves droop.

Fear

Does fear have a hold on us? Do we fear the pain of being misunderstood? Are we afraid to be open and honest, to be "me," because we accuse ourselves of many wrongs? The truth is: *The heart is deceitful above all things and desperately wicked (Jeremiah 17:9).* I'm glad God doesn't ask us to trust our heart.

Are we afraid someone will hurt us worse than we've already been hurt? Or maybe we're afraid to even try, lest we fail again. Many hurting people struggle with fear.

Pride can also keep us from trying. It's okay if things don't always turn out the way we planned. In many things we have another chance.

Fear at the root of a trampled flower can be like the air we breathe. There seems to be no getting away from it. Maybe someone seldom trusted us to do anything right. Is there maybe a deeper pain that seems too embarrassing to tell? Pray about it and seek to share with someone who will allow openness to talk about deep wounds.

Honesty is important. Tell Jesus about the fear that controls you. He wants to confirm His love and take away that fear. Mustering up strength of our own brings on fear. But with faith eyes fixed on Jesus there are untold resources to our needs.

Confusion

Everything feels topsy-turvy. We've tried to organize life but it doesn't seem to work. How can we make life less disappointing and confusing?

When efforts to work through the mists of our journey seem to fail, we may again accept wrong thought patterns. Did God ask us to get every wrinkle out of life before we can be happy? No. Did He ask us to trust Him? Yes. What does God want of us while this spiritual battle is raging? He wants us to desire His righteousness with all our heart.

Truth doesn't change. Commit yourself to God. He will give rest on that firm foundation—Christ Jesus. He is worthy of our trust in a confusing world. The drooping leaf of confusion can be refreshed again! Be earnest and open with God, and be willing to share with someone if the need be.

Sad Blossoms

Strong opinions

A girl can have strong opinions about things. And this isn't all bad. We need to have a strong hold on God's truth.

One day I was talking with a young boy I know and love deeply. He was making strong, negative remarks about someone. We got into a brief argument, and in defending that person, I said to him, "Don't worry your little head about it." Immediately, I regretted my insensitive words to him.

Had I been more gentle and allowed God to refine my opinion, I would have said what was deeper in my heart. Then I might have said, "The one you are talking about is dear to my heart, and I love her as I love anyone else."

Gentle words would have influenced my listener's heart more than the hasty words I spoke.

Sometimes we try stating strong opinions to hide how badly we feel about ourselves. Are we making strong opinions to feel better about ourselves? We should take time to consider why we feel strongly about things. When we consider others and how they feel, the outcome is better relationships.

Search your motive when expressing opinions. God cherishes the beauty of gentleness.

Hating myself

We never really hate ourselves, but sometimes it feels that way. It seems like nothing good is left inside and hatred seem reasonable.

A girl can lash herself inwardly because of her past, making her bruises go even deeper. In her rejection she tries her best to perform the task before her, but it leaves an aching void in her soul. *I'm no good. I can't do anything right. They don't really like me.* **The Great Healer wants to make the difference in her life.**

What happens when we start noticing others' needs and feelings? Try to focus more on the interests of those around you. Good things happen inside when we care about others. Thinking about others leaves less time to look negatively at ourselves.

Losing self control

Did you ever have a day when nothing seems to go right? We all experience them, everything seems out of control. Nothing goes the way we planned. In times like this it's easy to get upset. We expect too much from others, then in our disappointment we speak unkindly or distance ourselves from them. Maybe we feel like giving up, or even hurting ourselves.

How can we be calmed inside?

The drooping spirit can be refreshed by focusing on God. There is a battle in the unseen world to destroy our peace, but His power is stronger than the fiery darts of the enemy. The enemy says things like, you can pray but God won't hear you. Your heart is not right. You failed. God is far away. With the shield of faith we can quench those attacks. *Ephesians 6:16*

In times like this I've looked to God, honestly and openly saying, "I've had enough trying on my own. It's all yours," and stillness resided in my soul. God wants our trust. He knows every detail of our lives and can release us from the toil and

A Trampled Flower can rise again

effort to control the fierce battle. He is in control of the entire universe, so He is much better able to take care of our world than we are!

Hurting others

What do we do when we hurt inside? One girl was hurting inside and feeling badly about a mistake she had made. It made her feel so frustrated that she kicked her favorite cat. Do we ever hurt our best friends? Have we said unkind things to them or maybe ignored them simply because we felt so bad inside? 1 Corinthians 13 is not only beautiful poetry but a beautiful life. Sometimes we need to retrace our steps to reconcile relationship.

What are our words and feelings towards others. Are they kind and loving? Does talking kindly to them make a difference in how they respond to us? Kindness makes life cheery—like bright sunlight on a flower.

Loneliness

Where are my friends?

When our life looks like a drooping flower, friends can be hard to find. The deep-down pain from abuse can make us want to withdraw from others.

Loneliness is often a result when we dwell on our problems.

Maybe a girl looks so confused, fearful, or opinionated that others feel uncomfortable. Unknowingly or not, this girl's thoughts are revolving totally around herself, so she shows little consideration for others' feelings.

When we accept the normal sorrow of life, knowing the perfect is waiting for us in heaven, we can more easily accept and understand the pain which others face. We are not alone in the fight for the right.

Jesus said, "Do to others as you would have them do to you." What could my friends do that would make me happy? Wouldn't my friends like if I did the same for them?

Building good relationships takes away our loneliness. It causes hearts to bloom. People are attracted to radiance!

Goodness
Faith
Virtue "Better Things"
Obedience
Self Control
Love
Joy
Patience
Gentleness
Purity
Kindness

Jesus
the Son

Self
Acceptance

Affirming Others
Making Good Comments

BELIEVING TRUTH

Suffering
for Jesus

Hiding Scriptures
in your heart

Jesus' Example
Acceptance
God's Presence
God's Light
God's Promise

...*A Light* that shineth
in a dark place, until the
day dawn, and the day star
arise in your hearts.
II Peter 1:19

Chapter Ten
What Love Does

Strength of Truth and Its Influence

Self-acceptance
the flower of Love and Joy

We are special to God! We know this is true.
"For I know the plans I have for you,"
declares the Lord, "plans to prosper you
and not to harm you, plans to give you
hope and a future" (Jeremiah 29:11 niv).

It may not be easy for me to forgive myself.
Maybe I don't easily stack up grudges against
others, but am I unforgiving about my own
blunders? I must be kind to myself and allow

myself the opportunity of trying again. I must understand that I'm subject to mistakes just like everyone else—we all need time to grow and mature.

Jesus said, "*Love your neighbor as you love yourself.*" When I forgive, I let God into my heart. His love allows me to accept others and myself despite mistakes.

"Then you will call upon me and come and pray to me, and I will listen to you. You will seek me and find me, when you seek me with all your heart. I will be found by you," declares the Lord (Jeremiah 29:12-14a niv).

God is wondrous Love. His very heart is Love. Fall into His loving arms. God is Forgiveness. He accepts an earnest, seeking heart immediately—He doesn't wait until we've done some worthy deeds.

When Jesus comes into an open heart, however, change begins. The love within us results in action. Others can walk by and see and smell the sweetness of the Christ-like heart.

A Trampled Flower
can rise again

Suffering for Jesus
The flower of Obedience, Self-Control, Patience

Sometimes people offend us or sin against us. It happens to everyone. When we refuse to let hatred and revenge into our heart for a misdeed… is not this how we suffer for Jesus? Can we show kindness in return when someone is hateful and selfish to us? Can we still love them? We can pray that God would help them to understand His love. Even when we are sad, we can pray for the people who are hard to love.

This is what Jesus did to people who mistreated Him. He is our example of love, and He makes it possible for our life to bloom in love.

And let us consider how we may spur one another on toward love and good deeds (Hebrews 10:24 niv).

Affirming Others
The flower of Purity, Kindness, Gentleness

Everyone wants to hear encouraging words. Think how encouragement comes by saying the right words. We can thank a Sunday school teacher for teaching an interesting lesson or take flowers to someone who is lonely.

A godly girl desires to be pure, kind, and gentle. She wants to bless others. She thinks about what she can do to make someone smile.

If I practice putting Jesus first, others second, and myself last, what kind of day will I have?

J-O-Y-ful!

Hiding Scriptures
in your Heart

The flower of Virtue, Goodness, Faith

When we love someone very much, we like to hear them talk. We love to read the letters and notes they write to us.

Who is speaking to me when I read the Bible? It is God! The Bible is the only book whose words have marvelous power to make bad people good, completely turning them around to a new life.

By believing and obeying Jesus' words, one's life can be changed. The soil of our heart is being prepared to grow good things when we allow it to soften in the Master's hands. Good things such as love and respect can bloom in our life.

There are comforting promises in the Living Word. There are stories and examples of times when God answered prayer. Jesus spoke kindly with wisdom to all. Welcoming God's Word into our life inspires our faith and enhances our walk.

For thou hast magnified thy word
above all thy name (Psalm 138:2b).

God's Word is Truth. Virtue will be the reward
of all who love His Word.

And he shall be like a tree planted by the
rivers of water, that bringeth forth his fruit in
his season; his leaf also shall not wither, and
whatsoever he doeth shall prosper (Psalm 1:3).

There are three ways we can hide God's promises in your heart. Read, memorize, and tell.

Add verses to this list that speak to your heart.

Let the heart of them rejoice that seek the Lord (Psalm 105:3).

I will praise thee: for thou hast heard me (Psalm 118:21a).

And they that know thy name will put their trust in thee: for thou, Lord, hast not forsaken them that seek thee (Psalm 9:10).

Be not afraid of sudden fear (Proverbs 3:25a).

Perfect love casts out fear (I John 4:18 nkjv).

God hath not given us the spirit of fear; but of power, and of love, and of a sound mind (II Timothy 1:7).

For the Lord shall be thy confidence, and shall keep thy foot from being taken (Proverbs 3:26).

The fear of the Lord is to hate evil: Pride, and arrogancy, and the evil way...do I hate (Proverbs 8:13).

But unto you that fear my name shall the Sun of Righteousness arise with healing in his wings (Malachi 4:2a).

O send out thy light and thy truth: let them lead me (Psalm 43:3a).

Hope in God: for I shall yet praise him, Who is the health of my countenance, and my God (Psalm 43:5b).

A Trampled Flower can rise again

Chapter Eleven
Right Thoughts

You understand all my thoughts
(Psalm 139:2 gnb*).

Through our Struggle, Jesus Cares Deeply

The unpleasant part of our past can influence us to keep thinking negative thoughts. Living with right thoughts will make life more pleasant for us and those around us.

Being honest about our heart and our thoughts brings God's truth and freedom into our life. What are we thinking today? Are we following lies or believing truth. Jesus said, "The truth shall make you free!" (John 8:32).

---

*Good News Bible

Wrong thought
Right thought

1. I'm scared to talk. People will think I'm weird.
"Jesus, I trust you to understand me even when no one else seems to."

2. What I said was good, but I could have done better. I'm not as intelligent as other people.
I did my best. "Lord Jesus, it matters most what people think about You. Use me to please You."

3. I'm so mixed up from my abuse; everything I say or do seems to get messed up. I feel ugly and no-good.
Jesus loves the real me. "Thank you, Jesus, for loving me when I hurt and struggle. Thank you for holding me close to You."

4. Nobody loves me. Poor me; everyone wants to do their own thing. Nobody cares about my feelings.

Feeling sorry for myself only makes me feel lonely and weak. I will reject self-pity. What can I do to make someone happy?

5. If I do enough things—give a toy to a child, pick up a pencil for someone, or be a good helper to my friends and family, Jesus will love me better.

Jesus loves me just the way I am. I can't do anything to make Him love me more.

6. Jesus is too busy to help me.

Jesus has no waiting room like a doctor has. "Thank You, Jesus, that you are in every place at all times."

7. Someone hurt me. I wish something bad would happen to that person.

Jesus is peace and love, and that is what I want in my life. "Help me, Lord, to forgive the one who has made my life so sad."

8. I'm going to do as I please and follow the lusts of the flesh so I can forget my sadness and feel better.

Following my own sinful desires will never make me feel better. Jesus can change my heart to make it good. I can please Him by choosing to do good things.

9. I want a friend just for me and no one else.

Good friends will help shape my character. "Jesus, you are my own personal unchanging Friend!"

10. I never want to see my abuser again.

If I ever see my abuser again, I will keep my heart right. I will stay close to someone I can trust, and thank God for His love that holds me close to Him.

11. I will never talk to my abuser again.

If I need to talk to my abuser, I will be confident God has taken me into His care, and will say words out of self respect that fit the occasion.

12. God isn't in my life now because I can't feel Him. I feel all torn and frazzled with weights of a hundred things.

God loves me now. I can't trust my feelings. My life is in the hands of the unchanging God. I will worship the Lord who has made me and is on this journey with me.

A Trampled Flower
can rise again

Chapter Twelve
Living to Worship God

One thing have I desired of the Lord, that will I seek after: that I may dwell in the house of the Lord all the days of my life, to behold the beauty of the Lord (Psalm 27:4).

Worship is a Way of Walking

David's desire was to be in the Lord's presence, always. He wanted to know God's direction and comfort, always. He wanted to see the Lord's beauty in everyday circumstances. His love for God moved him to serve God all the days of his life.

How much do we love God? Is His beautiful character the desire of our heart?

Many thoughts pass through our mind each day. Sometimes it's hard to remember what is most important. The most important thing in life is to know who God is. David knew this in truth. We can learn with David to "behold the beauty of the Lord."

In the next lines, there are thoughts to ponder. Read them slowly. Think about these truths as you seek to know who God is and how great His love is for you.

How can I see the beauty of the Lord in each day?

With eyes of faith I can see
Him and know Him.

How can Jesus be my joy in everyday life?

Gaze on the beauty of Jesus
and see His unfailing love.

Realize that every good and perfect
gift I receive is from God.

How can I give Jesus priority in my thoughts and emotions?

Admire His loveliness. Allow Him to crush my ugly selfishness.

Desire and yearn for Him. Give Him first place in my heart.

Glory only in Him—He is the One who enables me to do right.

Be awed at God's power to do the impossible. Arise from the dead!

His power makes it possible for me to be part of His loveliness.

Admire the beauty of Jesus' patient love for me.

Be patient with myself when I seek words to express my heart.

He never gives up on me.

Look to Jesus, who turns no one away.

As I look at His beauty, I will become more like Him.

Love is a flame. Christ's love for
me is unquenchable—it never
dims, and casts out all fear.

Reverence Him for His forgiving love.

Endless, forgiving love is the best
part of God's goodness!

I may come boldly to the throne of God with
all my needs (Hebrews 4:16).

Know Him who gives peace to the desperate.

He dwells in my heart because I choose to let
Him be Master of my life.

He is compassionate and accepts
all the love I feel for Him.

I give Him my first affection and let
Him rule on the throne of my heart.

Look to Him and be overcome
by His constant love.

He wants me to be His forever!

Grace is something I don't deserve
or earn, but He favors me and
wants to give all His benefits.

Worship is looking to God and
seeking what He wants for my life.

Worship is thanking God for
all His goodness to me.

All people worship something. My life is
most rich when I worship my Father, God.

A Trampled Flower
can rise again

Appendix

Dear Trampled Flowers,

Being a young girl, your foremost question might be, *What is God's plan for me?* Your awesome Creator has a special plan for you.

The unknown can look big to you, but you have a great big God to trust with your all. If you live and work for Him today, he will make a plain path for you tomorrow. Change and growth are part of everyone's life, and God will stay close to you every step of the way.

God chooses when and how our future will unfold, and He is much more capable to plan it than we are!

You cannot always see your inward maturity but God is faithful when life's lessons are the hardest; He'll see you through. He plans each step of your life with the goal of making you more like Himself.

In our part of the world, the accepted age for maturity is eighteen. Children younger than that are protected by the law. Thus an older person is in trouble with the law if he or she has sexually violated anyone under the age of eighteen.

Why are these teen years protected? This is a special time of your life. You are discovering who you are. Your body is making fast changes as you mature. You may sometimes wonder if you are a girl or a woman. Your body and soul are going through the swirling cycle of change into the beauty of womanhood. It is sometimes bewildering and exciting, but this is the process of becoming an adult.

You may feel like a stranger to yourself. One day you feel like reaching for your limits and the next moment you feel like climbing into a small, safe box. Your emotions do flip-flops. Emotional swings from high to low aren't bad. They are part of not being a little girl anymore. God is doing a good work in you. He designed each stage of your physical, emotional, and spiritual growth.

It can look frightening, not knowing what your big, open future holds. In these years of rapid change, you will long for something secure that won't change. You can quickly trust in something that looks and feels secure.

Someone may want to rob you of your purity. Because you want security and don't have an adult's awareness, you might not detect someone's evil intentions. This is one reason why older people choose to trick young people who are confused or unsure about sexual boundaries.

If someone wants to use your body for sexual pleasure, please ask someone for help. First, ask God to walk through this valley with you. God never intended that His children walk alone in their sorrow.

God can show you how to see and understand what happened to you. Please don't blame yourself for being sexually abused. Instead, look to God's understanding and healing.

Ask God to help you find a caring Christian to share your experience with. Don't be afraid to share your painful memories in detail. It will be hard to think about those bad memories, but it takes more energy to cover pain than to share it. When God allows sorrow into your life, He is making room in your heart for greater joy than before.

Be thankful for help and guidance from Christian parents and other caring adults in your life who want to share God's love with you. When you accept their love, you are building a strong tower that can protect you later when your life seems to be crumbling. These teenage years are setting a foundation for you to build stronger relationships.

Toward the end of your teen years, you will likely feel more stable emotionally. You will have stronger convictions about right and wrong. You'll be able to look back and see that God was taking care of you in younger years, and that His love and faithfulness never change.

We are all born in sin and need a new heart. If you have given your heart to Jesus and have Him as the Master of your life, you have His wonderful companionship. Even if your future looks dark, He knows everything and knows each step ahead of you. This is the best security you can have!

What does God want from us? Micah 6:8 explains what God requires of us: *to do justly*—see things as God sees them, to be honest and fair; *to love mercy*—give others room to grow because we are learning too; *to walk humbly with your God*—looking to Jesus, not ourselves or others.

Today your character is taking shape. You want your character to please God and bless others.

You are a beautiful young lady designed by God. No matter what is in your past and no matter what is ahead of you, God is still with you, shaping you. He wants to reveal His beauty through you so people can see what a great God He is. No matter who you are, you are His treasure!

Walking with Jesus,

–*Lena M. Martin*

Dear One, (the abuser)

I want to talk with you if you suggested or carried out abuse to another. This book will help you too. You have brought pain and conflict into your own life. By reading you can see the damage this has done to yourself and another.

You belong to God. He wants you for His own. Pray from the bottom of your heart for God's work in your life. His love reaches to your need as well as anyone else's. You can turn around and live for Him. Be as honest as you can.

Share with someone who loves God wholeheartedly. Someone who can go with you to talk to the one you have hurt. God will give you a new beginning. God's love is stronger than wrong. God bless you.

Walking with Jesus,

Lena M. Martin

A Trampled Flower
can rise again

Dear Friends of Trampled Flowers,

You may know a young girl who is living in the aftermath of abuse. She needs someone to whom she can open her heart and share what is in her heart. Use this book as a tool to help you understand her, and for her to understand herself better.

Prepare your heart in prayer as she courageously breaks through the wall of raw emotions that engulfs her. The Great Physician said, *Where two or three are together in my name, I am there with them.* When you are together, invite and recognize the presence of the Lord Jesus in audible prayer. Ask for His power of healing to the struggling girl.

What were the needs of the children brought to Jesus? He tenderly held them close and blessed them. No doubt many of those children felt emotional healing from bitter experiences when His gentle hands touched them. The loving hand of the Great Healer is still extended to the young girl suffering emotional trauma.

It is very important that the recovering girl knows that being molested as a child made her a victim. She doesn't trust her own judgment. She must hear from you that she is not guilty and that God's love for her is as real as ever. Believing in this love will give her confidence to trust the Father heart of God.

Your young friend may suffer severe loneliness. She wants to be part of the free world around her, but feels locked up in hopeless despair. When she knows she can trust you, you could ask, "Is something hurting you? Something you find hard to talk about?"

If she can't talk about it, you might encourage her to write about her pain. Assure her that Jesus can touch her broken heart. His compassionate heart is worthy of her trust. God wants to do great, incredible things in her life!

The silence that hides the abuse needs to be broken. Failure seems to stalk her, and to talk about the abuse makes her feel dirty again. She will come to you feeling devalued, disrespected, and fearful of pressure. She may feel trapped because her abuser controlled her with threats

to do worse things if she ever told anyone. She needs to respect others, but she is so full of pain there seems to be no place left for respect.

Your helpful support will enable your young friend to express herself. Even if she may only be able to say, "I can't explain how I feel," or, "I am worthless and stupid," or, "I can't trust anyone and don't fit in anywhere," it is a start.

Combined with prayer and God's presence, talking about the abuse is the only way to unlock the door and begin a new journey to wholeness.

If the abuse remains bottled up, it turns into a poison that will destroy her emotional freedom and rob her ability to trust people. Locked-up pain results in a confusing mass of anger and fear. Only when the abuse is brought out into the open will the stress be relieved. Talking about it prevents the abuse from owning her, and she will not own it anymore either.

Even when you get her to accept and claim the Shepherd's love and truth, she may again feel fearful several days later.

Let her feel Christ's grace and patience. Let her know that she can choose Jesus to be her refuge, and that His love for her will remain strong during this time of growing. Offer hope.

God's love and care is beautifully shown in Jeremiah 23:4. *I will set up shepherds over them which shall feed them: and they shall fear no more, nor be dismayed, neither shall they be lacking, saith the LORD.*

It is important to forgive the offender. This will help clear the burden of the offense. Someone needs to be with the girl if she consents to see the offender. It may be best for the offender to know the pain, anger, and fear he or she brought to the girl. She need not go to length, but tell clearly the damage, and forgive her offender. Don't expect or insist on many words from the offender. That must come as a result of the offender's own decision.

It is important for the girl to forgive herself. An unforgiving attitude can go unnoticed and greatly hinder a free spirit. For her to know the Father heart of God, forgiveness to herself must be sought and found.

May God bless praying, mature people who ask questions and listen to the heart of young people. The Good Shepherd cares for His hurting lambs. This book was written prayerfully and with tears—with the compassion that comes from the Good Shepherd Himself.

Lena M. Martin

Additional Resources

Joy for Mourning
By: Anne Miller

A personal testimony of healing from childhood sexual abuse

Beauty for Ashes
By: John Coblentz

Biblical help for the sexually abused

Available from:

Christian Light Publications, inc
P.O. Box 1212 · Harrisonburg VA 22803-1212
Telephone: 540-434-8896